A Campaign in New Mexico
with Colonel Doniphan

A Campaign in
New Mexico with

COLONEL
DONIPHAN

Frank S. Edwards

Foreword by Mark L. Gardner

University of New Mexico Press
Albuquerque

The Author Affectionately Dedicates This Work To His Mother

Originally published by Carey & Hart, Philadelphia, 1847.
Foreword © 1996 by the University of New Mexico Press
All rights reserved.
First University of New Mexico Press Edition

This volume faithfully reproduces the complete text of the first edition
published in 1847. Chapter abstracts have been moved to the end of the book. A
more recent map of the Missouri Volunteers' march replaces the original one
engraved by Thos. Sinclair of Philadelphia.

Library of Congress Cataloging-in-Publication Data

Edwards, Frank S.
[Campaign in New Mexico]
A campaign in New Mexico with Colonel Doniphan / Frank S. Edwards :
foreword by Mark L. Gardner. — 1st University of New Mexico Press pbk. ed.
p.   cm.
ISBN 0–8263–1698–0 (pbk.)
1. Doniphan's Expedition, 1846–1847—Personal narratives.
2. Edwards, Frank S.   I. Title.
E405.2.E26   1996
973.6´23—dc20   95-34100
                                                                         CIP

Contents

Foreword VII

Preface XXIII

Chapter One 3

Chapter Two 17

Chapter Three 35

Chapter Four 53

Chapter Five 69

Chapter Six 83

Chapter Seven 101

Appendix 119

Chapter Abstracts 135

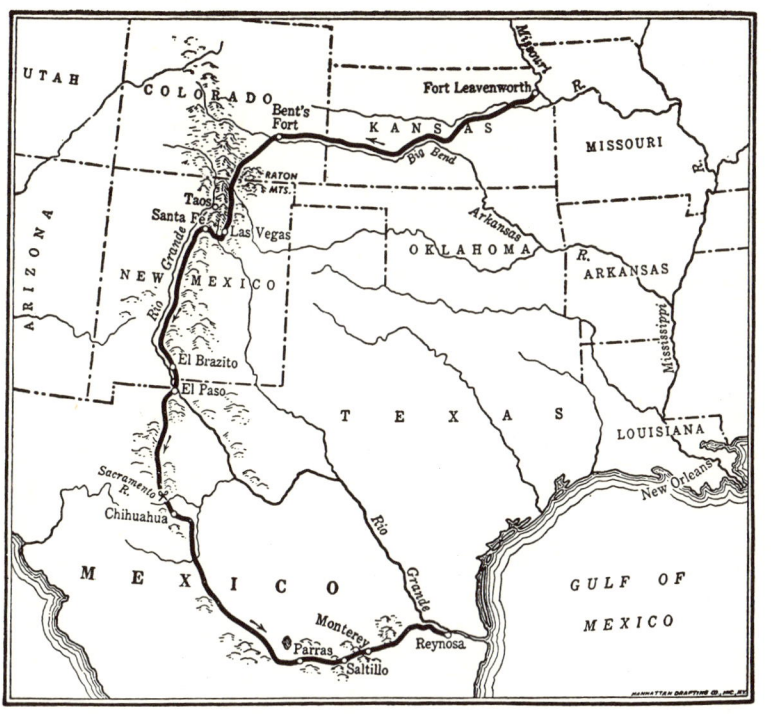

THE ROUTE OF THE MISSOURI MOUNTED VOLUNTEERS

(From Bernard DeVoto, "Anabasis in Buckskin: An Exploit of Our War with Mexico," *Harper's Magazine 180* (March 1940), 400–410.)

FOREWORD

By Mark L. Gardner

IN MID-JUNE of 1847, in the midst of the Mexican–American War, Colonel Alexander W. Doniphan and his small, ragged army of Missouri volunteers arrived in New Orleans, straight from a sensational campaign that had captured the imagination of the American people. In twelve month's time Doniphan's command had marched the length of the Santa Fe and Chihuahua trails and won, singlehandedly, two battles against Mexican armies, one against dramatically superior numbers. These volunteers, at the time amounting to slightly more than eleven hundred men, had alone conquered the State of Chihuahua, Mexico, whose population was estimated at one hundred fifty to one hundred sixty thousand. Their expedition was "an achievement," wrote Secretary of War William Marcy, "to which it would be difficult to find a parallel in the history of military operations."[1]

The exploits of Doniphan and his Missouri volunteers had been reported in newspapers across the country, from the New Orleans *Picayune* to the New York *Evening Post*. There were few indeed who were not aware of their epic march. Now the Missourians appeared at New Orleans in the flesh, and, once again, failed to disappoint. The New Orleans *National* wrote that Doniphan's

officers and men . . . have a strange, uncouth appearance: Piecemeal, the ill made clothing of the volunteers has fallen from them, and they have supplied its place with what chance and the wild beasts of New Mexico have thrown in their way.

VII

VIII • FOREWORD

Their sun-burnt faces, grizzly beards, and withal their devil may care air, is perfectly irresistible. Yet beneath those rough exteriors, are concealed minds of educated and high toned sentiments, full of lofty thoughts and love of liberty—minds that are destined to be felt in the councils of the nation, and to play a prominent part in the stirring events of the times.[2]

Doniphan and his volunteers, now bonafide media darlings, were mustered out of the service at New Orleans before making their way home to countless banquets and barbecues held in their honor. Among those receiving an honorable discharge on June 24 was one Francis S. Edwards. Frank (the name he seems to have preferred) was in St. Louis early the following month, where he made out an application for bounty land due to veterans.[3] He then appears to have headed for home, which was located not in Missouri but New York. Frank must have been extremely busy for the next several weeks, for by the middle of November, the Philadelphia publishing firm of Carey & Hart had printed his "thin volume," *A Campaign in New Mexico with Colonel Doniphan*—an amazing feat accomplished without the benefit of word processors, fax machines, or laser printers.

Frank definitely had good marketing sense. Prominently featured in the title was the name of his picturesque commander Colonel Doniphan, who had emerged as a national hero nearly on a par with old Rough and Ready himself, Zachary Taylor. Three other books, hurriedly issued that same year and the next by fellow campaign veterans, also took advantage of Doniphan's name: John T. Hughes's *Doniphan's Expedition . . .*, William H. Richardson's *Journal of William H. Richardson, a Private Soldier in Col. Doniphan's Command*, and Jacob S. Robinson's *Sketches of the Great West: A Journal of the Santa Fe Expedition, under Col. Doniphan....*[4]

Coming out in fall 1847, Frank's book was what we would today call the perfect Christmas gift, unless, of course, one preferred

FOREWORD • IX

Victor Hugo's *The Iron Mask* or Ned Buntline's *The Magic Figurehead*, both of which, at twenty-five cents, sold for half as much as *A Campaign in New Mexico*.[5] But considering the enthusiastic reviews, his book was well worth the extra two bits. "It is simply what it purports to be," commented the New York *Evening Post*,

> a narrative of the personal adventures of the writer and his comrades in the campaign made by Doniphan and his brave men . . . . These are related in that simple and natural manner which convinces the reader that no exaggeration has been used, and which begets a deeper and more continued interest than could be awakened by any embellishment.

"It is worth reading," wrote another reviewer. "We get from it a very vivid notion of that astonishing Mexican war." *Godey's Lady's Book* was also taken with the volume, proclaiming it "one of the best Mexico–Texan books that have as yet been issued."[6]

What is perhaps the most insightful evaluation comes from the pages of *The Merchants' Magazine and Commercial Review*:

> Of all the narratives touching Mexico, and the events growing out of our difficulties with that Republic, written and published during the last eighteen months, this is the most interesting to us, from the fact that its pages are not entirely occupied with accounts of blood and carnage, and the horrors of the battlefield. Mr. Edwards has embodied, in an agreeable form, his observations during part of a campaign with "the Xenophon of the nineteenth century," and given us many interesting incidents, besides a fund of information connected with the habits, manners and customs of the people of New Mexico. The work is written in a chaste and scholarly, but unostentatious style; and is doubtless a faithful narrative of the circumstances and events of the campaign. It deserves, and we trust it will find a wider circle of readers, than the many catch-penny glorification "histories" of the events, and of the "heroes" engaged in this anti-Republican, anti-Christian war.[7]

x · FOREWORD

The stinging last sentence of this review is a jolting reminder that not all Americans supported the conflict with Mexico.[8]

A Campaign in New Mexico apparently sold well in the bookstores, for it was reprinted in 1848 and again in 1849, and an edition was issued in London in 1848. These volumes are now extremely collectible in the rare book world. Recently, a first edition of the work, in its original paper wrappers, was offered at $1,250.[9] The only printing since 1849 has been a "Readex Microprint" issued in 1966, which itself is out of print. Obviously, a reasonably-priced reprint is long overdue. Yet it is not simply the book's limited availability that has brought about the present edition. Actually, the reasons for republication can be found in the reviews above, for what made Edward's account of value 150 years ago still holds true today for both the scholar and aficionado. For those interested in the nineteenth-century American Southwest, the Mexican War, and the Santa Fe and Chihuahua Trails, his brief narrative indeed offers a "fund of information."

Frank was wonderfully observant and had a sharp sense for things worth writing about. But readers should be aware that he was an impressionable young foreigner who at times found local stories and rumors irresistible—which, in some ways, makes his account that much more interesting. A particularly bizarre passage in his book concerns the Pecos Pueblo ruins and its defunct Spanish mission, now a national historical park. Frank writes, "There are many traditions connected with this old church, one of which is that it was built by a race of giants fifteen feet in height, but these dying off, they were succeeded by dwarfs with red heads, who, being in their turn exterminated, were followed by the Aztecs." Frank was apparently inclined to believe the tale, for he saw an excavated thighbone which, he was convinced, "could never have belonged to a man less than ten feet high."

Another eye-opener awaiting those familiar with New Mexico history is Frank's unique theory on territorial governor Charles Bent's death at the hands of Pueblo Indians and Mexicans during the Taos revolt of January, 1847. Frank came to the conclusion that the insurrection "was used as a cloak to cover what was, undoubtedly, an act of private malice, instigated by his wife." He was of course wrong; Bent was killed because he was an American, as were others unfortunate enough to be in Taos at the time, and Bent's wife (cohabitant, actually) was in real danger herself. Frank's account of the manner in which Bent was killed is also erroneous, all of which is understandable. His information about this affair came secondhand (he was several hundred miles to the south when the Taos revolt erupted). The reader will find that Frank is much better with things he experienced personally—with the exception of giant thighbones.

And Frank experienced plenty: pesky gnats and gusts of wind like "a blast from a furnace"; buffalo meat cooked over a buffalo chip fire ("I . . . would rather have a piece of good beef"); gambling at monté ("The mysteries of the game can only be learnt by losing at it"); the stirring battles of Brazito and Sacramento; and more. Frank was on hand as one of the more controversial episodes to come out of the Mexican War unfolded. About midnight on August 16, 1846, he was aroused from his bedroll by the appearance in camp of a sergeant with an important prisoner, and, his curiosity getting the best of him as usual, he accompanied the pair to General Stephen Watts Kearny's tent. The prisoner, a son of Captain Dámaso Salazar, brought news that the Mexican army under Manuel Armijo, which had fortified itself at Apache Canyon, just outside Santa Fe, had dispersed. "[H]e assured us that our entry into Santa Fe would be bloodless," Frank wrote. And two days later it was.

Because many details concerning Armijo and the fall of New Mexico have come to light since Frank penned his account a century and a half ago, this enigmatic incident deserves fuller discussion here. According to Frank, young Salazar told the Americans that the Mexican army disbanded "in consequence of some quarrel about precedence in rank among the officers." It was later ru-

XII • FOREWORD

mored, however, that Manuel Armijo and his second-in-command, Diego Archuleta, had been "bought over" by Anglo trader James Magoffin, who with a detachment of thirteen dragoons had arrived in Santa Fe ahead of the American army in an effort to negotiate a peaceful takeover (Frank makes no mention of this entourage in his book). After the war, Magoffin did claim sole responsibility for the bloodless conquest in a letter to the War Department seeking compensation for his services, as Polk's special agent, in both New Mexico and Chihuahua.[10] And there were those close to the events who believed that the veteran merchant was indeed instrumental. In a letter supporting Magoffin's claim, Captain Henry Smith Turner wrote:

> Having been Chief of Gen[l] Kearny's Staff when he entered New Mexico in 1846, at the head of the Army of the West, I distinctly remember the services rendered by you to the Government, and to the General, in enabling the latter to accomplish successfully the object of that expedition: viz. the conquest of New Mexico *without bloodshed*, or *resistance on the part of the inhabitants*. This was much desired by our Government at the time; and I have no hesitation in saying, that the General was greatly aided in bringing it about, by your acquaintance with, and the influence you exercised over, the leading men of the Country.[11]

Captain Philip St. George Cooke, who was in charge of the dragoon escort, believed that Magoffin had persuaded Archuleta not to resist by advising him that the United States would only claim that area of New Mexico east of the Río Grande (which is what Magoffin understood at the time), thus leaving the country west of the river ripe to Archuleta's own imperial aspirations.[12]

But it is not as simple as all this. On August 12, in response to a letter from Kearny delivered by Captain Cooke, Armijo replied that his people had "risen *en masse* as an immoveable force to oppose the suggestion which Your Lordship has made me to surren-

FOREWORD • XIII

der the Department . . . and, honoring their expression and my duty as General, as Governor, and as a Mexican citizen, I am placing myself at their head." Armijo was willing to discuss matters further, but "without denying the rights of my country."[13] Then, on either August 14 or 15, Armijo ordered his military forces, approximately three to four thousand men (largely militia and some Pueblo Indians) to Apache Canyon, fifteen miles from Santa Fe.

Some historians have conjectured that these defensive preparations were a bluff, that he had no intention of fighting the Americans.[14] Yet it is still within the realm of possibility that Armijo was, at least for the moment, genuinely determined to oppose the invasion, only to change his mind later. Support for this scenario comes from an American who wrote the following at Santa Fe some months afterwards:

> It appears, from accounts I have received of persons who were on terms of intimacy with Armijo, that from the time he learned that Gen. Kearny was on his march to Santa Fe, he could hardly be said to be of the same mind from one day to the next—at times fiercely bent on resisting the Americans, and then the fever would leave him in a most wretched state of despondency and indecision.[15]

At Apache Canyon the "fever" left Armijo for good, although accounts of what happened there are just as contradictory. According to a report signed by over one hundred citizens of New Mexico, Armijo told the militia at Apache Canyon that "he would not risk facing battle with people lacking military training" and ordered them home. The Mexican commander then declared his intention to meet the American force with his regulars but promptly fled south with these after the militia disbanded. Armijo, on the other hand, claimed in his report that the militia "did not want to offer any resistance because they did not have supplies or artillery, and that they did not wish to sacrifice themselves uselessly and fill their country with more calamities." Armijo then asserts that the

XIV • FOREWORD

militia deserted him and that he and his officers subsequently decided to join their small force with that of the commandant-general of Chihuahua.[16]

Whatever happened at Apache Canyon, and whatever was behind it, the abandonment of this defensive position by Armijo left the door to Santa Fe wide open. The Army of the West marched down the capital's dusty streets on August 18, the American flag was raised over the Palace of the Governors, and Stephen Watts Kearny claimed New Mexico for the United States. Residents of Santa Fe, Frank writes, feared that the Americans would "rob and ill-treat everybody and destroy everything." As the army occupied the city, "sobbing and crying were heard from the houses."

The reader will find that Frank minces no words when describing the Mexican people. Like nearly all of his fellow soldiers, he brought with him a hefty dose of intolerance and racist contempt. Frank's negative depictions were likely primed, in part, by two popular works published just a couple of years before the outbreak of the war: Josiah Gregg's *Commerce of the Prairies* and George Wilkins Kendall's *Narrative of the Texan Santa Fe Expedition*, both of which portrayed Mexicans in an unflattering light (Gregg's book is actually referred to in Frank's text and Kendall is mentioned as well). It is also obvious that some of Frank's biases stem directly from the culture he was a part of, a culture that believed Anglo-Saxons to be superior to races of darker complexions. For instance, when speaking of Mexican women, Frank found only those with "much white blood in them" to be pretty.[17]

But while Frank, like the majority of nineteenth-century Americans, was not as enlightened as we would like him to be, one should be careful not to dismiss his observations out of hand. A case in point is Frank's portrayal of the Mexican Catholic clergy, particularly in New Mexico. He conducted business with priests while serving as the quartermaster sergeant on the Chihuahua expedition. More than once, he suspected the priests of attempting to cheat him when he was purchasing commissary supplies from their

FOREWORD • XV

stocks. Frank was also disgusted by what he saw as the immoral lifestyle of the priests and their poor treatment of parishioners. Although some critics might quickly ascribe this to simple anti-Catholicism, there is strong evidence that some New Mexicans actually shared Frank's sentiments.[18]

It is worth noting that Frank did not reserve his criticism for Mexicans alone. He surprisingly narrates an incident in which his well-liked commander, Alexander Doniphan, failed to discipline a soldier for stealing a pig from a "poor Spaniard." The soldier bluntly admitted the deed to the colonel while the pig's owner looked on. "I am afraid the complaining party got no redress," Frank commented. "I felt it to be a bad example." Frank was most appalled, however, by what he learned of the brutal acts perpetrated by the Texas Rangers. After one ranger narrated to Frank their technique (a rope around the neck) for extorting supplies and money from Mexican *hacendados*, Frank remarked, "Who can wonder at the Mexican becoming a guerilla?"

At this point it might be wise to say something about Frank himself, the outspoken author of this absorbing little volume. From his book we gather that he was from New York. Other than that fact, he offers no clues to his background. From census records we learn a little more: that Frank was born in England and that he was nineteen years of age at the time of his enlistment in 1846.[19] The date of his arrival in the United States, the names of his parents, his education—all this is unknown. However, from his book we discover that he admired the poetry of William Cullen Bryant, that he read Walter Scott, and that he spoke French. Frank offers no explanation for being in St. Louis when the war broke out—just that he happened to be there. He does provide one of his motivations for volunteering, though: "to obtain the restoration of my health, which had been, for some time, very much impaired." It may have been that weak health prompted his journey westward in the first place.

Frank, along with "some of the first young men of the city," joined a company of horse artillery being organized by the dashing Richard Hanson Weightman, who was esteemed for having attended West Point, although he had not graduated. Weightman's company was accepted into the service as Company A of the Battalion Missouri Light Artillery, which was commanded by Major Meriwether Lewis Clark, a genuine West Point graduate and a son of explorer William Clark. Frank's company furnished their own uniforms, which were made "similar to the fatigue dress of the regulars." These "consisted of a flat blue cap with red band bearing the artillery emblem, short blue jacket with red standing collar, and trousers with red stripes—one stripe for the men and two for the officers."[20] The volunteers who had formed companies from the rural counties up the Missouri River jeeringly referred to Frank and his fellow St. Louisans in the Army of the West as the "City Pets."

Shortly after the army marched off from Fort Leavenworth at the end of June 1846, Frank was to experience a singular western phenomenon known as the "prairie cure." "[W]hen I bade adieu to St. Louis," Frank writes, "I hardly expected to get across the prairies alive. But I had not been a week upon them before I felt that my whole being was changed, and ere I reached the settlements, I was one of the most robust of the whole company."[21] Frank was one of the lucky ones. The enlistment of many other volunteers for the same reason had been, in the words of Lieutenant Richard Smith Elliott, "a most fatal mistake." Elliott continued, "The army is no place to repair a shattered constitution. It is true that such a trip as we have had is pretty certain either to kill or cure the patient, but the chances are sadly in favor of the first issue."[22]

One intriguing episode in Frank's military career is not recounted in his book. Recorded on his certificate of war service in the Missouri State Archives are the following brief lines: "Deserted at Santa Fe, N. M., Oct. 8, 1846" and "Deserted from hospital after being ordered by surgeon to report for duty on discharge from hospital, October 8, 1846."[23] Frank makes no mention of having stayed in the hospital or of having been ordered to serve there. How this incident was resolved is a mystery, but his "desertion" was appar-

FOREWORD • XVII

ently not considered serious, for Frank continued his volunteer service in the field.[24] The following month he was one of a limited number of men selected for a choice assignment.

On November 17, the commander of American forces in Santa Fe, Colonel Sterling Price, ordered Lieutenant Colonel D. D. Mitchell to open a communication with the army of General John E. Wool, supposedly marching on Chihuahua, and to select an escort of one hundred men from the army in Santa Fe. Mitchell was instructed to choose men "with reference to their efficiency, intellectual and physical."[25] Frank applied for the duty and was one of nine selected from Captain Weightman's company.[26] Furthermore, he was appointed the quartermaster sergeant for the expedition. Mitchell's detachment left Santa Fe on December 1 and soon overtook Colonel Doniphan's First Regiment Missouri Mounted Volunteers at Valverde, approximately 157 miles south of Santa Fe. Doniphan had been ordered by General Kearny to report with his regiment to General Wool in Chihuahua. Mitchell's detachment thus continued as a part of Doniphan's command, and as such, Frank and his comrades would share in its adventures and laurels.

While it is best to let Frank tell the story of the "campaign," something should be said in regard to the significance of Doniphan's expedition. Wool, of course, was not in Chihuahua (his orders had been changed after he and Zachary Taylor decided that the capture of Chihuahua was unnecessary), and the six-foot two-inch Doniphan took it upon himself to conquer the Mexican state with his own small army. He did so in spectacular and commendable fashion. Unfortunately, this conquest, which Frank helped immortalize, had little, if any, bearing on the outcome of the war. Richard Smith Elliott probably summed up the campaign best when he wrote years later that "apart from its glory, there was no great result, except to show how large a scope of country could be conquered without strength enough following to hold it."[27]

As previously mentioned, Frank's book was issued in November 1847. He was twenty years old at the time (Lewis Garrard,

XVIII • FOREWORD

another young author of classic Western Americana, was twenty-one when his volume, *Wah-to-Yah and the Taos Trail,* was published three years later). According to surviving records of the publishing firm of Carey & Hart, *A Campaign in New Mexico with Colonel Doniphan* was issued in a total first edition of four thousand copies (both cloth and paper), evidence of the publishers's confidence in the volume's sales potential. Fifty review copies were sent out to various magazine, journal, and newspaper editors. The total cost for this first press run was $499.86.[28] What Frank got in royalties is unknown, but since the book did see more than one printing, they must have been worth his effort.

After the publication of his book, Frank next turned up in 1848. During the month of January he wrote a supporting statement for merchant Manuel X. Harmony, who then had a claim before Congress for wagons and goods that Colonel Doniphan had commandeered near El Paso del Norte.[29] The following year our young author is listed in *Trow's New York City Directory* for 1849–1850 as a druggist at 907 Broadway.[30] Frank is thenceforward found annually in various directories for New York City through 1861, the last to which I had access. His profession is given as druggist or chemist until 1851; then, in *The New York City Directory* for 1852–1853, his vocation is given as "agent," although it is possible that this designation was an error. In a directory for 1854–1855 Frank was listed for the first time as a physician, and he continues with that respected title in all subsequent directories.

Frank is found in both the 1850 and the 1860 U. S. censuses. In the first he is a druggist, twenty-three years of age, and he has a wife, Catherine, twenty-one years of age. In the 1860 census he is, as expected, recorded as a physician, but his wife's name is here given as Elizabeth, and she is twenty-nine, which *suggests* that Frank remarried sometime during the interim (census takers made mistakes also). Listed with Frank and Elizabeth is their two-year-old daughter, Ella, and all three are living in the household of a forty-two-year-old music dealer by the name of Thomas Goodwin.

FOREWORD • XIX

Unfortunately, at this point, the trail of Frank S. Edwards ends, at least for the present. He is not found in the soundex for the 1880 U. S. census for New York, and no pension record exists for his Mexican War service. Had he lived long enough, he almost surely would have applied for a pension. Several questions remain unanswered. Did Frank, like many of his fellow comrades, take part in the War of the Rebellion? He was young enough, and certainly his medical skills would have been valued. And if Frank's life was indeed cut short, was he revisited by his fragile health, absent too long from the salubrious climate of the western plains? It is hoped that with more digging, these questions can someday be resolved.

In the preface to *A Campaign in New Mexico with Colonel Doniphan*, Frank writes of laying his "imperfect account of the expedition before the public." One hundred and fifty years after the outbreak of that "anti-Republican, anti-Christian war," the University of New Mexico Press has placed his book before the public once more, and thankfully so. But I have a bit of a quarrel with the title; I think it should be "A Campaign in New Mexico with Frank," for that is what the book truly is. The personality of this young druggist, his way of seeing things—that "devil may care air"— ranks this book a cut above similar accounts and earns it a place among the classics of the literature of the nineteenth-century West. It was Frank's only book, but he could not have written a more valuable one.[31]

Notes

1. From Marcy's official report as quoted in the St. Louis *Daily Reveille,* December 17, 1847.

2. As reprinted in *Nile's National Register,* July 17, 1847.

3. Francis S. Edwards Bounty Land File, 4363-160-47, Bureau of Pensions Correspondence and Pension and Bounty Land Case Files, Record Group 15, National Archives, Washington, D.C.

xx • FOREWORD

4. See Henry R. Wagner and Charles L. Camp, *The Plains & the Rockies: A Critical Bibliography of Exploration, Adventure and Travel in the American West, 1800–1865,* ed. Robert H. Becker (San Francisco: John Howell, 1982).

5. Advertisements of W. H. Graham and Berford & Co. in *The Evening Post* (New York), December 6, 1847.

6. *The Evening Post* (New York), November 26, 1847; *Littell's Living Age,* December 9, 1848; and *Godey's Lady's Book* 36 (February 1848): 131–32.

7. *The Merchants' Magazine and Commercial Review* 18 (January 1848): 127.

8. See John H. Schroeder, *Mr. Polk's War: American Opposition and Dissent, 1846–1848* (Madison: University of Wisconsin Press, 1973).

9. "Special List: The Mexican War," catalog of William Reese Company, New Haven, Connecticut, 1995.

10. Magoffin's claim and most of the accompanying documents were first published in William E. Connelley, *A Standard History of Kansas and Kansans,* 5 vols. (Chicago: Lewis Publishing Company, 1918), 1: 123–35.

11. H. S. Turner to J. W. Magoffin, St. Louis, January 14, 1849, James W. Magoffin Papers, Western History Department, Denver Public Library, Denver, Colorado. This letter has somehow eluded students of the Magoffin claim and, as far as I can determine, has not previously been published.

12. Connelley, *A Standard History of Kansas and Kansans,* 1: 134.

13. Max L. Moorhead, ed., "Notes and Documents," *New Mexico Historical Review* 26 (January 1951): 81–82.

14. See Daniel Tyler, "Governor Armijo's Moment of Truth," *Journal of the West* 11 (April 1972): 307–16; and John P. Wilson, "The American Occupation of Santa Fe: 'My Government Will Correct All This,'" in David Grant Noble, ed., *Santa Fe: History of an Ancient City* (Santa Fe: School of American Research Press, 1989), 97–113. Tyler believes that Armijo had made up his mind to abandon New Mexico "no later than August 3."

15. Jared W. Folger to Messrs. Keemle & Field, Santa Fe, January 13, 1847, in the St. Louis *Weekly Reveille,* March 22, 1847.

16. Moorhead, ed., "Notes and Documents," pp. 73 and 77.

17. A good synopsis of American soldiers' attitudes towards Mexicans is found in James M. McCaffrey, *Army of Manifest Destiny: The American Soldier in the Mexican War, 1846–1848* (New York: New York University Press, 1992), 66–79. For soldier impressions of New Mexico specifically, see John P. Bloom, "New Mexico Viewed by Anglo-Americans, 1846–1849," *New Mexico Historical Review* 34 (July 1959): 165–98. Bloom found that the works of Gregg and Kendall were influential in many of the writings he examined.

FOREWORD • XXI

18. See particularly the comments of Antonio Barreiro in H. Bailey Carroll and J. Villasana Haggard, eds., *Three New Mexico Chronicles* (1942; reprint ed., New York: Arno press, 1967), 53–55. See also David J. Weber, *The Mexican Frontier, 1821–1846: The American Southwest Under Mexico* (Albuquerque: University of New Mexico Press, 1982), 76–79; and Joseph P. Machebeuf as quoted in W. J. Howlett, *Life of the Right Reverend Joseph P. Machebeuf, D.D.* (1908; reprint ed., Denver: Register College of Journalism, 1954), 164–65.

19. Seventh U.S. Census for New York, New York City, 9th Ward, 165; and Eight U.S. Census for New York, New York City, 16th Ward, 2nd District, 1021.

20. V.M. Porter, "A History of Battery 'A' of St. Louis," *Missouri Historical Society Collections* 2 (March 1905): 5.

21. Santa Fe trader and author Josiah Gregg had a very similar experience. See his *Commerce of the Prairies*, ed. Max L. Moorhead (Norman: University of Oklahoma Press, 1954), 23–24.

22. St. Louis *Daily Reveille*, January 1, 1847.

23. Private Francis S. Edwards Certificate of War Service, Missouri State Archives, Jefferson City, Missouri.

24. The muster roll for Company A of the St. Louis artillery battalion, in the National Archives, Washington, D.C., contains additional brief details about Frank's service. The most tantalizing is a remark concerning Frank's service during the period November–December, 1846: "Lost Carbine, Bucket, Screwdriver, & Wiper." I am indebted to historian Brian Pohanka for this reference.

25. Order Number 71, Headquarters, Army in New Mexico, Santa Fe, as reprinted in George R. Gibson, *Journal of a Soldier Under Kearny and Doniphan, 1846–1847*, ed. Ralph P. Bieber, Southwest Historical Series, vol. 3 (Glendale, Calif.: Arthur H. Clark, 1935), 371.

26. St. Louis *Daily Reveille*, February 20, 1847.

27. Richard Smith Elliott, *Notes Taken in Sixty Years* (St. Louis: R.P. Studley & Co., 1883), 246.

28. Carey & Hart Cost Book #3, page 41, in Box 98 of Edward Carey Gardiner Collection, Historical Society of Pennsylvania, Philadelphia.

29. See U.S. Congress, House, [Report on petition of] *Manuel X. Harmony*, H. R. Rep. 458, 30th Cong., 1st sess., 1848 (Serial 525), 31. A second, undated, statement by Edwards is found on page 43 of this report.

30. U.S. History, Local History and Genealogy Division, New York Public Library, to Mark L. Gardner, New York, New York, December 13, 1994. If Frank was trained as a druggist before his service in the Missouri Volunteers, it

XXII · FOREWORD

might explain the order requiring him to report for duty at the hospital in Santa Fe. Also, *Green's St. Louis Directory (No. 1) for 1845* (St. Louis: James Green, 1844) contains an advertisement for Edwards & Francis, Apothecaries and Druggists. The Edwards of the firm name is Lewis Edwards. Could this be a relative of Frank's? Frank, by the way, is not listed in any St. Louis directories of the period.

31. Out of justice for Frank, one more item pertaining to his book needs to be mentioned—a fantastic case of plagiarism. In 1970 an "1851 journal" written by a Josiah Rice was published under the title *A Cannoneer in Navajo Country*. The "journal" purports to document Rice's journey down the Santa Fe Trail and service in New Mexico territory under Colonel Edwin Vose Sumner. Yet nearly half of the "journal" is lifted almost verbatim from sections of *A Campaign in New Mexico;* only the names of officers and a few places have been changed. Rice's Santa Fe Trail trip, with the exception of a few paragraphs, is completely Frank's, and many of Frank's observations on New Mexico are scattered throughout the rest of the bogus document. Frank's table of distances for the Santa Fe Trail has also been appropriated. That Frank's book would be used in such a way is somewhat fascinating, but it is most regrettable that this very serious problem was not detected before *A Cannoneer* was published. See Richard H. Dillon, ed., *Journal of Private Josiah M. Rice, 1851: A Cannoneer in Navajo Country* (Denver: Old West Publishing Company, 1970).

Colonel Richard Hanson Weightman

Weightman was the captain of Edwards's artillery company. (Portrait from Ralph E. Twitchell, *The History of the Military Occupation of the Territory of New Mexico from 1846 to 1851 by the Government of the United States* [Denver: The Smith-Brooks Company, 1911].)

Alexander W. Doniphan
Edwards's light artillery company was attached to Colonel Doniphan's Missouri volunteers. (Portrait by George Caleb Bingham, ca. 1850, courtesy State Historical Society of Missouri, Columbia.)

TO ALL WHOM IT MAY CONCERN.

Know ye, That *Francis S. Edwards*, a *private* of Captain *Weightman's* Company *A* in the Battalion regiment of *Missouri foot Light Artillery* volunteers, who was enrolled at *St Louis Missouri*, on the *8Th* day of *June* 1846, in the Company then commanded by Captain *Weightman* and mustered into the service of the United States, at *Fort Leavenworth* on the *19Th* day of *June* 1846, by *Capt James Allen 1st Dgn* to serve for the term of twelve months, from the *19Th* day of *June* 1846; and having served, honestly and faithfully, to this present date, and the said company having been, this day, mustered for discharge, is hereby **HONORABLY DISCHARGED** from the said service, by reason of the expiration of the term for which the company was mustered therein.

Given at *New Orleans La.* this *24Th* day of *June* 1847.

Signature of Commanding Officer.

R. H. Weightman

S. Churchill

Commanding Company.

Insp. Gen. & Mustering Officer.

Frank S. Edwards's Discharge Paper
This certificate shows that Edwards's discharge was honorable. (Bounty Land Warrant Files, National Archives, Washington, D.C.)

"John W. H. Patton," Missouri Volunteer
Missouri volunteers were the majority of the Army of the West. (Sketch
courtesy Museum of New Mexico, Santa Fe, negative no. 147638.)

Charge of Captain Reid at Sacramento
(Sketch by Lachlan Allan MacLean, pen and ink and graphite on paper, 198.166,
Amon Carter Museum, Fort Worth, Texas.)

The Battle of Sacramento, 28 February 1847 (Lunette by Fred G. Carpenter courtesy Missouri State Museum, a facility of the Missouri Department of Natural Resources' Division of State Parks.)

Monument to Colonel Alexander W. Doniphan, Courthouse Yard, Richmond, Missouri
(Bronze statue by Frederick C. Hibbard erected by the State of Missouri in 1918; photograph by Mark L. Gardner, 1995.)

PREFACE

THE AUTHOR cannot better introduce his work than by giving a copy of an article from the New York Evening Post, which its senior editor, William Cullen Bryant, Esquire, kindly allows him thus to use:

XENOPHON AND DONIPHAN.

"These are the names of two military commanders who have made the most extraordinary marches known in the annals of the warfare of their times. Col. Xenophon, as in modern phrase he has justly a right to be called, lived about one hundred years earlier than the Christian era. Born in Greece, and educated under Socrates as a favorite pupil, he, at the age of nearly forty years, joined a regiment of Greeks, who had enlisted under Cyrus the younger for a campaign, as it was pretended, against the Pisidians, but, in reality, against Persia, as the Greeks soon discovered after their march had begun. The object of Cyrus, as our readers well know, was to dethrone his brother, the King of Persia. After a long march through Asia Minor, Syria, and the sandy tract east of the Euphrates, the two brothers met at Cunaxa, not far from Babylon. Cyrus fell in the almost bloodless battle that ensued, his barbarian troops were discouraged and dispersed, and the Greeks were left alone in the centre of the Persian empire. The Greek officers were soon massacred by the treachery of the Persians. Xenophon stepped forward, and soon became one of the most active leaders; and, under his judicious guidance, the Greeks effected their retreat northward

XXIII

across the high lands of Armenia, and arrived at Trebisond, on the southeast coast of the Black Sea.

"From thence they proceeded to Chrysopolis, opposite Constantinople. Both Colonel Xenophon and the regiment, consisting of about five hundred men, were greatly distressed, having lost almost everything excepting their lives and their arms. The length of the entire march of the Greek force, as nearly as we can now estimate it, was three thousand four hundred and sixty-five English miles. It was accomplished in fifteen months, and a large part of it through an unknown, mountainous and hostile country and in an inclement season. The history of this march has survived the ravages of two thousand years; and, as one of the best productions of a Greek scholar, is now used as a text-book in our schools.

"Turning now to the wonderful march of Colonel Doniphan, we find the first regiment of Missouri mounted volunteers mustered into the service of the United States at Fort Leavenworth, on the sixth of June last year, and, on the 22d of the same month, they commenced their march across the plains for Mexico. After a march of fifty-seven days' duration they entered Santa Fé. On the 16th of the present month," (June, 1847,) "we find this regiment at New Orleans, about to be discharged, as their enlistment for a year was nearly expired. In the mean time this body of men has fought three battles, viz., Bracito, Sacramento and El Poso. That of Bracito was on Christmas day, and opened an entrance into El Paso del Norte. The Mexicans had twelve hundred and fifty men and one piece of artillery; the Americans four hundred and twenty-five infantry—the piece of cannon was captured, and the Mexican army entirely destroyed. That of Sacramento was fought on the 28th of February. This battle—one of the most remarkable in the war—is familiar through the reports of Col. Doniphan and other field officers. The battle of El Poso was fought about the 13th May, by the advanced guard under Capt Reid—the Americans had twenty-

PREFACE • XXV

five men and the Camanches sixty-five. The Indians were routed, and left seventeen bodies on the field. Three hundred and fifty head of cattle, twenty-five Mexican prisoners, and a great deal of Mexican plunder were captured.

"The battle of Sacramento lasted three hours and a half; and the slaughter of the Mexican army continued until night put an end to the chase. The men returned to the battle-field after dark, completely worn out and exhausted with fatigue. The Mexicans lost 300 men killed on the field, and a large number of wounded, perhaps 400 or 500, and 60 or 70 prisoners, together with a vast quantity of provisions, several thousand dollars in money, 50,000 head of sheep, 1,500 head of cattle, 100 mules, 20 wagons, 25 or 30 carts, 25,000 lbs. ammunition, 11 pieces of cannon, mostly brass six pounders, 6 wall pieces, 100 stand of arms, 100 stand of colors, and many other things of less note.

"This body of men conquered the states of New Mexico and Chihuahua, and traversed Durango and New Leon. In this march, they travelled more than six thousand miles, consuming twelve months. During all this time not one word of information reached them from the government, nor any order whatsoever; they neither received any supplies of any kind nor one cent of pay. They lived exclusively on the country through which they passed; and supplied themselves with powder and balls by capturing them from the enemy. From Chihuahua to Matamoras, a distance of nine hundred miles, they marched in forty-five days, bringing with them seventeen pieces of heavy artillery as trophies.

"It must be confessed, that in many very important particulars, these two expeditions differ from each other. One was the march of a conqueror, the other was the retreat of an inferior force. One was made on horseback, and the other on foot and at an inclement season of the year. One was made at an early age of the world, when military science was undeveloped, the

XXVI · PREFACE

other was made with all the advantages of modern improvements. But our object is not so much to draw a comparison between these two expeditions as to notice the circumstances that these two men, whose names are in sound so similar, have each performed the most wonderful march in the annals of warfare. If Col. Doniphan will now imitate the example of Col. Xenophon, and give to the world as charming and as perfect a history of his expedition as the latter has done, mankind, two thousand years hence, will admire and honor him."

In the absence of such a charming and perfect work from Colonel Doniphan, a young volunteer lays this imperfect account of the expedition before the public.

A Campaign in New Mexico
with Colonel Doniphan

Chapter One

WHEN the Texian revolutionary army, after their many victories under the command of General Sam Houston, halted on the banks of the Rio Grande, a council of officers was called, to determine what should be the boundary of the new republic. All the officers present, with the single exception of Houston, advised that the chain of mountains, lying about one hundred miles west of the Rio Grande, should be adopted as the western boundary line: thus embracing the rich and thickly-settled valley of the river; but Houston overruled their decision, and insisted that the river itself should be the line, from its mouth on the Gulf of Mexico, as far north as the 39° of latitude, from thence eastwardly, taking the old boundary of the state of New Mexico as far as the Arkansas River, which it was to follow to the 100° of longitude, thence directly southward to Red River, and, after following the windings of which for some distance, to run along the western boundary of Louisiana to the Gulf.

The line proposed by the junior officers of the council would have embraced the whole of the states of New Mexico and Coahuila, as well as Texas—while that insisted on by Houston, and which was finally adopted, divided each of the former about the middle. The object of carrying the line so far north at the western corner of the Territory, was in order to include the rich valley of Taos, which contains, among other places, the city of Santa Fé, well known as the headquarters for the immense trade which is carried on, by means of caravans, between the northern

4 • A Campaign in New Mexico

parts of Mexico and the United States. This trade is principally managed by citizens of Missouri, where all these trading expeditions are fitted out and dispatched.

The Texian government had enough to occupy them in resisting the incursions of Mexico in the south, and, therefore, could not find time to subjugate the more northern part of their territory. So that this part remained, until the year one thousand eight hundred and forty-six, in the possession and under the dominion of the Mexican government; and although, when Texas was received as one of the United States, it was accepted with the boundary which I have stated, yet, not until the numerous annoyances of the Mexicans had forced our government to post, on the banks of the Rio Grande, the "Army of Occupation," was the important trade carried on between Missouri and Santa Fé considered worthy of protection, and, then, only in connection with the plan already determined upon for the opening campaign in Mexico.

The governor of New Mexico, Manuel Armijo, had subjected the American traders to numerous extortions; for instance, collecting a duty of five hundred dollars on each wagon load of goods. Now this, as the goods mostly sold by them were the coarser kinds, was a serious imposition.

To remedy this state of things, and also to carry out a very important part of the plan of operations resolved upon by our government in its then warlike position against Mexico, the President of the United States ordered General Kearney, and old and tried officer, whose achievements in Florida are known, to raise a sufficient number of volunteers, although not to exceed three thousand, which, being united with such regulars as might then be at the post on the Missouri river called Fort Leavenworth, were to form an army to be called the "Army of the West." With this small body he was to cross the western prairies and take possession of New Mexico, making Santa Fé, which is the capital, the centre of his operations.

This expedition was not unfraught with danger: not only were the troops to cross nearly one thousand miles of uninhabited prai-

CHAPTER ONE • 5

rie, subject to annoyance from hostile Indians, and run the chance of starvation should their supplies of food be, by any means, cut off, but they were ordered to hold the country, after they had conquered it, well assured that no reinforcements would be sent out. General Kearney was also empowered to proceed to California after subjugating the Mexicans.

He, in obedience to these orders, called upon the Governor of Missouri for one thousand volunteers, to be raised from the different river counties of the state.

One battalion, to consist of two companies, was to serve as light artillery and the rest as mounted riflemen. The Governor, in apportioning out this requisition, called on the county of St. Louis to furnish the separate battalion of artillery, dividing the rest of the draft among the several counties north of it.

Perhaps no place could be found which would so readily respond to such a call as St. Louis: for, it being the point where the Santa Fé traders procure their goods, it is a common thing to observe their arrival with numerous packages of specie, which they freely use in making their purchases. This naturally gives the idea of vast mines of gold and silver at Santa Fé; and the young men of all classes were eager to go—indeed, it became a question who must be left; as, besides gold and silver and visions of flowery prairies, buffalo hunting and Indian skirmishing, General Kearney was well known to be a kind officer to his men, although a strict disciplinarian—and Richard H. Weightman, a gentleman of St. Louis, who had received his education at West Point, although he had never yet seen service, no sooner declared his intention to form a company, than his list was filled by some of the first young men in the city. Happening to be at St. Louis, and my time hanging heavily on my hands from unusual inactivity, I obtained an introduction to Mr. Weightman, and was so much pleased with his frank open countenance and gentlemanly bearing that I speedily enrolled myself in his corps. The service was to be for one year or for a less period if found expedient. Each soldier was to furnish himself with a good horse, saddle, clothing—in short, everything except arms. Although we were not absolutely required to uniform ourselves, it was recommended that a suitable uniform would be desirable, so we provided a neat dress, somewhat similar to the fatigue dress of the regulars. We also got our Spanish saddles all made of one pattern. The common but good article we procured could hardly, strictly, be called a saddle, as it consisted of nothing but the skeleton or tree of one, with the girth and stirrups attached. The object of the simplicity was to render it as light and cool as possible to the horse; and, by putting a good Mackinaw blanket above as well as beneath, it made a comfortable seat—the blankets forming our beds at night. Our horses were good, being principally Illinois grass-fed animals, just suited to the service for which they were now wanted. Mine carried me more than two thousand miles in the Mexican country, and he was, at last, stolen from me at Saucillo, about eighty miles below Chihuahua, and I almost felt I could have cried when, after long search, "Old Tom" could not be found. An important part of our equipment was a stout leathern waist belt, supporting a good butcher-knife, to which many of us added a revolving pistol, a weapon we found very useful. And knowing that we should be obliged to go over long distances without finding water, we all provided ourselves with tin canteens holding half a gallon:—these, covered with a piece of blanket, kept wet to cool the water, are a very necessary article.

Numerous stories of Indian massacres and cases of starvation on the prairies were told to us by our friends, in the hope to deter us from going; and all this was increased by an old Canadian hunter named Antoine, one of our company. He was a genuine specimen of a Rocky Mountain hunter, and nothing seemed to please Antoine better than to get a knot of us "green-horns" around him, questioning about prairie life, and to give us the most discouraging answers. It was not done from a bad motive, but, seemingly, in a kind and considerate manner; and yet he did evidently delight to paint everything to the inexperienced in the worst possible view. However, Antoine had been a great traveller, and, so, was privileged.

CHAPTER ONE · 7

When we arrived at Fort Leavenworth, we were received into the service of the United States. We were detained at the fort until the end of the month of June, by the non-arrival of our cannon, which were daily expected from Springfield. For some time previous and during our stay, every second or third day would witness the departure of long trains of government wagons, which, loaded with provisions, were dispatched with orders to push on as fast as possible to Bent's Fort, a trading post about five hundred miles on the road, there to await our arrival.

After numerous delays, on the 30th of June, 1846, we started on our long journey; and not very encouragingly, for we left our captain ill at the fort, and, therefore, went under the command of the first lieutenant. This cast a shadow on our spirits, as Weightman was a great favorite. The first day's journey was uninteresting, as we only marched eleven miles, and much of this was through the farm attached to the fort. Our whole battery, embracing the pieces of the company commanded by Captain Fisher, consisted of eight long brass six pounders and two twelve pound howitzers; and to each of these, as well as to the caissons, were harnessed four fine dragoon horses. But many of these had never felt harness before, and, at first particularly, gave us much trouble; and, on the second day, when we came to and forded a beautiful stream, running through a narrow belt of timber, we found it almost impossible to get our teams to pull together, and it was, at last, found necessary to dismount the men and have them drag the cannon up the muddy bank.

From where I stood, on the opposite side, my attention was drawn to one of the prettiest *coups d'oeil* I ever saw. Below me, plunging and kicking, were the horses attached to the pieces, surrounded by the men, and, on the opposite side, seen through the trees and shrubbery, were the rest of our company in their bright and gay uniforms, grouped around their shining cannon, appearing along the winding path which led down the high steep bank of the stream. The sun was almost totally excluded overhead, and the warmth of coloring thus given to the scene rendered it truly beautiful.

When we emerged from this belt of trees, the first prairies met our view. The grass was as high as the backs of our horses, and grew so rank as to render it almost impossible to make our way through it, except just in the road. We found it sprinkled with flowers which, although neither so beautiful nor so abundant as I had anticipated, gave it a pleasing appearance which we missed in the prairies that we afterwards passed. Perhaps it is one of the most beautiful sights in nature to see a puff of wind sweep over these grassy plains, turning the glistening sides of the grass to the sun, and seeming to spread a stream of light along the surface of the wave-like expanse. And a sight of these prairies would often cause Bryant's beautiful lines to rise to my lips, and I would picture to myself the magnificent plains peopled by the almost extinct red man—his leaving for a wider hunting-ground—and fancy, with the poet and his murmuring bee—

"The sound of that advancing multitude
Which soon shall fill these deserts. From the ground
Come up the laugh of children, the soft voice
Of maidens and the sweet solemn hymn
Of Sabbath worshippers."

Here, by a mistake of our guide, we lost the California emigrants' path; but, on crossing a high roll in the prairie, we found out our mistake, and, after much difficulty, got into the right road again.

About forty miles from the Fort, the Kansas or Kaal river crosses the road, and, on reaching it, we found a regular ferry established by government and managed by two Indians. This is one of the most beautiful rivers I ever beheld; and although but a quarter of a mile across, it is very deep in some places, but clear as crystal, sweeping rapidly along between high rocky banks, and, at last, emptying itself into the Missouri, a few miles above Independence.

On its banks, near our camp, in a bark cabin, I saw a beautiful and nobel-looking Indian woman—a beauty of that order which might command admiration rather than affection. Her fine black eye shone as she observed our admiring gaze; but she continued swinging her child, which, tied to a piece of bark, hung from the roof by a thong of deer's hide, without deigning to return our notice of her. By the side of the cabin, on a freshly-barked tree, were drawn, with charcoal, several Indian hieroglyphics. The whole scene, cabin, woman and papoose staring at us with its large eyes, realized one of Cooper's life-like Indian sketches.

We had hitherto been travelling what is known as the military road, and only struck the great Santa Fé road on the fourth of July, at what is called Elm Grove.

We now considered ourselves fairly on the great prairies.

How discouraging the first sight of these immense plains is to one who has read the numerous glowing accounts of them! how far short they fall of these descriptions, none can imagine who have not seen them!—only covered with a short poor grass in some parts, and, in others, producing nothing but a dry bushy plant or wild sage; they may be travelled over for miles and miles, without your finding bush or tree to obstruct or break the view. In many places it is so perfectly level, that you appear, when passing over them, to be travelling in the hollow of a might bowl; on all sides, the surface, although flat, appears to swell at the horizon, while you are apparently climbing up the side towards that edge which you never approach. But, oh, the breath of the prairies! When the breeze, which always rises at sundown, fans your cheek after a hot day's ride, you sink quietly to sleep, feeling that that soft delicious air is bringing health and strength to your weary body. How much I felt this can only be known to myself.—One of my reasons for going on this expedition was, to obtain the restoration of my health, which had been, for some time, very much impaired; and when I bade adieu to St. Louis, I hardly expected to get across the prairies alive. But I had not been a week upon them before I felt that my whole being was changed, and ere I reached the settlements, I was one of the most robust of the whole company.

At the Cotton-wood forks of the Neosho, where we encamped on the ninth, we were visited by a tremendous rainstorm, which

10 · A Campaign in New Mexico

soon flooded the bottom in which we were encamped. I can hardly imagine a more wo-begone looking set of men than we were the day we remained here. All the morning the rain poured down in torrents; not a particle of anything could we cook, but sat, wrapped in our soaking blankets, in our little six feet square tents, which by no means kept out the rain, but rather sifted it and made it more penetrating, while around each tent we had thrown up a small embankment, which prevented the entrance of the water. About noon the sun shone; and we, heroes, might be seen, crawling, one after the other, out of our canvas dwellings. At night, we lay down in our wet blankets on the muddy ground, and, in spite of the exposure, there were no colds complained of in the morning. We, of the city, had been considerably sneered at by the country volunteers, who called us "The City Pets," prophecying that the effects of our previous indoor lives would now be seen, but I can affirm that we, who had previously led what would be called by many a delicate life, had fewer cases of sickness, and less shirking of duty, than occurred amongst those young farmers whose whole lives had been spent in the open air, and of whom the other companies were formed.

The place we were now at is the same where the trader Chavis was so brutally murdered in 1843, by a party of land pirates. His grave lies just outside the belt of timber which skirts the stream. I, afterwards, while in Mexico, met with a young son of Chavis', about eleven years old, who had come to our camp to get medical advice for an uncle. In the course of conversation we asked him, knowing that he had been educated at St. Louis, how he liked Americans? His little eyes glittered, as he exclaimed, "When I am a man, I shall be a soldier; and then I'll kill every American I can. They murdered my father, and I'll pay them for it!"*

---

*How true to nature is Walter Scott? After writing the above, I came across the following passage in "The Monastery." "The trembling mother, half fearing as he spoke, drew the children towards her, one with either hand, while they both answered the stranger. 'I will not go with you,' said Halbert, boldly; 'for you are a false-hearted southron; and the southrons killed my father, and I will war on you to the death when I can draw my father's sword.'"

Captain Weightman arrived the night before we left this encampment. We passed on the 8th, the Lost Spring, so called on account of a remarkable difficulty in finding the exact spot where it rises. As we were moving out of camp in the morning, a light rain, which had been falling for some time, ceased, and the sun shone brightly out. The heat of its rays seemed to engender, from every blade of the wet grass, countless myriads of a small insect, bearing some resemblance to a gnat, which covered us and our horses so thickly that the original color of whatever they alighted upon could not be distinguished. Without biting, they got into the nostrils, eyes, and ears, creating a singularly pricking sensation, and making our horses almost frantic with pain. After an hour's annoyance, a light breeze arose and swept them away.

We arrived at Pawnee Forks on the fifteenth of July; and found the stream so high that we were forced to wait until the next day for it to subside. This stream runs very rapidly, between high, steep banks, and any slight rain on the mountains will make it rise so high in six hours that the traders are not unfrequently detained several days before it falls sufficiently to allow them to pass. Here, I first tasted buffalo meat. Our hunters, who were selected from the companies each morning, had been successful in killing three out of an immense herd which we had seen crossing a roll of the prairies during the day. There must have been three or four thousand in the herd, and, from the distance, they resembled a shadow cast upon the earth from a black cloud as it passes across the sun. The buffaloes killed consisted of two old tough bulls and a nice young cow—the latter of which, Antoine, our hunter, had taken; but, in the general arrangement of making all buffalo taken form common stock, we had to run the chance of our meat and only part of one of the old bulls fell to us, which made Antoine so angry, that he went to General Kearney and told him he would in future hunt for none but his own company;—as this was not allowed, he hunted no more. On account of the entire absence of wood here, we had to use the dry dung of the buffalo, called by the hunters *bois de vâche* or buffalo chips, for fuel. There was plenty of it around our camp, and it had one advantage over wood, it requiring no chopping. It makes a good and hot fire without flame, but had a strong ammoniacal odor, which is imparted to everything cooked by it. Our buffalo meat, which we simply roasted on the live embers, of course partook largely of this flavor, supplying the want of pepper, which our mess was out of. The part most esteemed by hunters is the small entrails, about a foot in length, and called by the delectable term, "marrow guts." These, although highly relished by the old hunters, never looked very inviting to me! To tell the truth, I was much disappointed in the flavor of buffalo-meat, and would rather have a piece of good beef.

The buffaloes, themselves, have the ammoniacal smell I have mentioned. This may, probably, arise from the earth which adheres to them after rolling in the mud where they stop, as the soil of the prairies is strongly impregnated with different salts. The mud-holes where they roll or wallow, become, sometimes, of very large size, from these living mud-scows carrying off, one after another, considerable quantities of the moist soil. The hunters call them "buffalo wallows." The rain forms them into ponds, and fish are frequently found in them—where do these fish come from?

A volunteer from one of the St. Louis companies was drowned during our stay at Pawnee Forks. He received a prairie burial; wrapped in his blanket and clothes, he was placed in his grave, and, without any form, it was filled up and covered over with stones, to prevent the wolves from meddling with the body.

We found the Arkansas River, which we struck on the nineteenth of July, very shallow; and this is frequently the case with its tributaries. They are sometimes dry; and then resort is had to digging a well in the bed of the river, in order to get water enough for cooking. It can thus always be found in abundance, by going down two or three feet, and it is always clear and cold.

Although the northern bank of the Arkansas is well covered with grass, and scattering groves of trees are not unfrequent, yet

Chapter One · 13

the southern bank consists of nothing but huge sand-hills, entirely destitute of vegetation. We had been travelling within sight of these hills for several days before we came to the river, and could hardly believe that we did not see large cities on the banks—indeed, we could plainly distinguish gilded domes of churches and roofs of houses,—the deception was caused by the rays of the sun upon the pointed sand hills.

While on our march along the banks of the river a singular phenomenon occurred. Towards the middle of the day, while no breeze was stirring, we were met by successive blasts of heated air, so hot as to scorch the skin and make it exceedingly painful to breathe; and these continued upwards of two hours. The sky, at the time, was entirely cloudless; but these gusts bore no resemblance to an ordinary current of wind, but rather to a blast from a furnace.

Although we had, by this time, arrived at the principal buffalo range, we saw but very few herds. The first sight of one of these animals at once shows him to be no easy customer to manage. The little glittering eye shines through the immense mass of long hair which covers the head and neck, giving the creature an exceedingly vicious appearance; while the contrast in size which is afforded between its hind and fore quarters adds materially to its hideousness, for he appears to be all head and shoulders, tapering off to the very point of the tail. Their pace, which is called by the hunters *loping*, is very singular, being a clumsy sort of gallop, but having the peculiarity of both fore feet being lifted off the ground at the same time and then both hind feet the same—giving the animal the motion of a ship in a heavy sea, first bows up, then stern. However, they manage to leave the ground behind them at a very rapid rate, and will frequently outrun a good horse. The best mode of hunting them is on horseback and with pistols. A horse that has been used to the chase will bring you close enough to almost touch the side of the buffalo, when you easily kill him by a well-directed shot behind the shoulder blade. At first a horse cannot be induced to approach one of these animals, and will ex-

14 • A Campaign in New Mexico

hibit the utmost terror when brought within scent of them; but after a few essays he is as fond of the sport as his master. As much depends on the truth of the first shot, a horse must know his business, for, by swerving at a wrong moment, he will cause the buffalo to receive only an irritating wound, and, in that case, the character of the chase is changed—the creature at once becomes a dangerous assailant, losing immediately all his previous fear of man and rushing to the attack with frightful bellowings.

Large gray wolves abound in all parts of the prairies and in Mexico, but particularly about the buffalo range. They are generally seen in packs, and will scent fresh meat or blood at a great distance; and being exceedingly cowardly they never attack man— and unless driven by hunger will not kill any animal, preferring dead carcasses. It was almost impossible to get any sleep during the night after we had killed any cattle, as these animals would assemble around our camp, and, sitting upon their haunches, howl in the most mournful manner all night long. Captain Fisher having been obliged to leave a sick horse behind one morning, sent back two men to kill him about an hour afterwards, his feelings for his tried steed making him wish to spare him further suffering. When the two men reached the spot where he had been left, a few picked bones, surrounded by a pack of snarling wolves, were all they found.

One night, while standing as sentinel on the outer side of our horses at the Big-timber on the Arkansas, I observed a man coming rapidly towards me, tossing his arms wildly in the air. I immediately levelled my gun and challenged him; and receiving no answer I was on the point of firing, when it occurred to me that it could not be an enemy, as no Indian would have acted thus, so I cautiously approached the man, who was now but a few steps off. I discovered it to be one of our own men, only partly dressed, and who had been seized with a fit, and was thus rambling unconsciously about. He had a truly narrow escape, as, had I acted strictly by my orders, I should have fired. I had hardly got him to his tent and again taken my post when daylight began to show itself. I was

CHAPTER ONE • 15

leaning upon my carbine, with my back to a small ravine along the edge of which my post extended and my mind in a quiet reverie, when, suddenly, from behind a bush, not three feet from me, a big gray wolf set up his dismal cry unconscious of my presence. It, annoyingly, took me by surprise;—snatching up a stone, I hurled it after his howling wolfship as he dashed precipitately down the ravine. I would have given something to have been allowed to shoot him, but as orders were to shoot nothing of less size than an Indian, I dared not alarm the camp by a shot.

In one of the country companies, called by us Grass-eaters or Doniphesians, two horses were shot by some frightened sentinel who had mistaken them for Indian warriors.

We saw but few Indians, and they carefully avoided us. All those bands that roam over the prairies have a great dread of cannon. This will account for their avoidance of us. They consider and call artillery thunder and lightning instruments. A band of them, a few years ago, attacked a party of traders who, besides their rifles, were armed with a small two-pounder cannon, which was fired with terrible execution upon their assailants. This taught them to respect artillery, and their fear has not subsided.

One evening, after encamping in a patch of timber, what was, apparently, a huge nest, was observed in the top of high tree, from which all the lower boughs had been cut. This, on close examination, proved to be a room constructed of buffalo robes among the branches, inside of which was laid in state the dead body of an Indian chief, while, under and around him were the finest skins and embroidered dresses, together with his arms and pipes. The air is so pure and dry in these plains that Indian bodies, thus deposited, do not putrefy. On Choteau's Island, two of our men found a dead Indian lying on the ground, which, by means of sticks, they made to stalk about the Island to the surprise and terror of some who were not aware of the motive power.

We passed by and over several prairie dog towns. One of these was very extensive, being three or four miles in circumference, and the ground shook under us as we crossed it, with a hollow sound, as if we were passing over a bridge. Although the name of dog is applied to these little animals, they bear no possible resemblance to our dogs, even their cry is most like a bird's chirp. They are much smaller than generally represented, being a trifle less in size than the common rabbit, and far superior to the latter in flavor. Between the skin and the flesh is a thick layer of fat which is a celebrated cure for rheumatism when applied as an ointment. We used it upon the sores on the backs of our horses occasioned by the chafing of the saddle, and it cured them at once. The old story of the rattlesnake and prairie dog associating together is now exploded, it having been proved that the former devours the pups of the latter, and that directly a snake takes possession of a hole it is, at once, deserted by its former inhabitant.

It was, by no means, an unusual occurrence for us, after a heavy dew, to kill, in the morning, within a quarter of a mile of camp, more than twenty rattlesnakes, which, having come out to imbibe the dew, had become benumbed by the cool night air and, so, were an easy prey. Our Major awoke one morning with one of these reptiles coiled up against his leg, it having nestled there for warmth. He dared not stir until a servant came and removed the intruder. I had now an opportunity of testing the truth of what I had heard, but never before believed: in the month of August only, these snakes are doubly venomous, but totally blind. An old hunter will tell you that the poison then is so virulent as to deprive the reptile of sight.

CHAPTER TWO

WE ENCAMPED on the 29th day of July about twelve miles below Bent's Fort. This was to be the rendez vous for the "Army of the West," and the first resting place since our march commenced. Hitherto we had had a sufficiency of both grass and water for our horses and provisions for ourselves. But our spies had just come in and reported that, beyond the fort, grass and water were very scarce; and General Kearney, in consequence of the scarcity of the provisions furnished for us, ordered that we should be put upon only half a pound of flour and 3/8ths of a pound of pork per day each man. This deprived us of coffee, sugar, salt, rice, &c., which had previously helped to make our provisions palatable. Now, our meals will consist of dough, if a simple mixture of flour and water deserves that name, fried in grease, or else what we used to call *slapjacks,* this being a thin variation of the aforesaid dough, poured into a hot frying-pan. Not very desirable fare; but we went to it jokingly.

Just above Bent's Fort we found all the traders who had started this autumn encamped, with the exception of the trader Speyers, who had hurried forward, having ammunition and arms with him to sell to the Mexicans. Though pursued by a party of our dragoons, he succeeded in reaching Santa Fé; and left again for the lower country. The traders generally had been ordered by General Kearney to here await his arrival. The troops which had come in amounted to one thousand seven hundred and fifty-seven; among them, were eight companies under Colonel Doniphan, consisting

17

of eight hundred and fifty men, and two companies of infantry. It will be seen that our whole number was small as an army; however, we were in good spirits. Nor were they damped by the following incident. A Mexican had been sent in, on some frivolous message to Captain Moore, (the officer who had gone after Speyers), with instructions to take *a good look* at the army. General Kearney, having discovered that this was the fellow's object, had the whole camp shown to him, and then dismissed him, with instructions to tell all he had seen to the governor of New Mexico. After going through the camp, he lifted up his hands, and, apparently in good earnest, exclaimed in Spanish, "Alas! for my poor country."

Bent's Fort is so named after the owners, (George and Charles Bent), who have long traded with Mexico and the Indians. It is merely a trading-post for the latter, and consists of a square of mud-houses, with a stockade around it. Here are kept the usual necessaries for the hunters who come and sell the skins they may have secured in the mountains around. These poor men are paid for their furs in goods, at most extortionate prices; for instance, they are charged twenty-five dollars for a gallon of brandy, while the New York price is two dollars. These hardy fellows, after having collected a sufficiency of furs and buckskins, bring them to the Fort, where, after bartering them off, they furnish themselves with a sufficiency of powder, lead and tobacco for another six months' trip to the mountains, and take the balance in whisky, with which they remain intoxicated as long as it lasts; and when it is gone, and all applications for more on credit are refused, they coolly shoulder their rifles and start off to do all the same thing over again.

At Bent's Fort we obtained a supply of draught mules to fill the places of the many horses we had killed by fatigue on the march—out of the hundred fine cannon horses with which we had started, not more than forty were left, and of these, not more than ten ever got to Santa Fé.

The Mexicans have always been justly celebrated for their dexterity with the lasso; and while crossing the prairies I had several

CHAPTER TWO • 19

opportunities of seeing a man in the employ of Bent, named Antonio, use it. He, having a very well-trained pony, boasted that he could hold anything, even a buffalo, with his nicely plaited lasso of deerskin, which always hung at the pommel of his heavily silver-mounted saddle. In holding an animal after he is noosed, the principal skill lies in the horse; who, as the lasso is fastened to the pommel of the saddle, unless very careful in properly bracing himself, will be overthrown by the sudden jerk.—One day, an old buffalo-bull passed near the wagon-train, and Antonio was told to show his skill on him. Proudly and confidently he started and threw his lasso, but, instead of catching the creature by the horns, as he should have done, he foolishly threw it over his head, thus noosing him round his powerful neck, The horse, seeing the lasso tightening, braced himself back; and, for an instant, it was a trial of strength between horse and buffalo; but the next moment, the bull was scouring away with the lasso, garnished with the silver-mounted pommel of Antonio's saddle, which had been torn off in the struggle.

Our time was too precious to allow us to linger here, and, on the second day of August, we again took up our line of march, leaving, just above the Fort, the Arkansas River, much to our regret; for on its banks we had always found a sufficiency of wood, water and grass. We started this morning, at eight o'clock, and were not out of the saddle until two o'clock the next morning; and then encamped by the side of some small salt ponds, entirely without either wood or grass, and the water so brackish as to be almost unfit for drinking. Our wagons not having come into camp with us, we none of us thought it worth while to await their arrival, but all lay down to sleep supperless. Never was anything enjoyed more by me than my sleep that night, except the next morning's breakfast. My bed, however, was only the ground with two blankets, and my saddle for a pillow, and my breakfast, salt pork and slapjacks.—I had not eaten anything since seven o'clock the previous morning.

20 • A CAMPAIGN IN NEW MEXICO

As we left the fort, the Rocky Mountains began to show themselves in the horizon, and, gradually, became more and more distinct. We had seen the snowy cap of Pike's Peak, the highest point north of the city of Chihuahua, the day before we reached the fort.

When we reached the foot of these mountains, I was disappointed to find them so entirely destitute of wood. They were bare, with no real beauty, aside from the grandeur inseparable from such enormous masses of rock and mountain, and although a few are covered with small firs, we crossed but one of these.

While encamped on the Rio Colorado, after crossing the first or Ratone range of the Rocky Mountains, I witnessed the coming up of a thunder storm among them, a sight not to be easily forgotten. We lay in a low valley, while, surrounding us, were immense peaks. Slowly, on all sides, great black clouds came rolling over the mountains, seeming too heavy to float, and sinking gradually down the sides. At last, when nothing could be seen around but these black clouds, shutting out the world from us, a long quivering roll of thunder echoed through the valley and the gates of heaven seemed to open on the mountains, for the rush of rain was almost confined to them—we receiving only scattering drops.

The first Mexican settlement was reached on the 13th of August, being a small village on the river Moro. It consisted of a few mud huts, and was called Lower Moro. Nothing could be more discouraging to men fated to remain a whole year in Mexican territory than the first view of this town. The houses or huts were built half underground, and consisted of but one room roofed with logs. In one of them I found a Scotchman, with his yellow wife and mongrel young ones. He owned large quantities of stock, and had several Mexican herders in his employ. He had made himself comparatively rich by supplying traders with mules and cattle. The few Mexicans who came around the camp certainly did not inspire us with any fear, but rather with disgust—swarthy, lean and dirty, in a few rags and with a torn old blanket around them, they were pictures of misery.

CHAPTER TWO • 21

The next day we encamped at a continuation of the same village, called Upper Moro. Here, the houses were a shade better, being entirely above ground, and several acres planted in maize. On an eminence stood a fort, which, the day before, had held a small force of Mexican soldiers, who had retired before us. However, our spies gave us to understand that a force of three or four thousand intended to attack us the next day in a narrow defile, called the Moro Pass, about a mile from the village. At this point the road, after passing between two high and perpendicular rocks, winds through hill and mountain for several miles. While we were at our scanty breakfast, our Major passing by, very gravely advised us not to eat too much, as we should fight the better for it. At this village, as at every other we entered, General Kearney delivered an address to the people through his interpreter, after the alcalde or mayor had taken the oath of allegiance to the United States.

The signal for mounting, called *boots and saddles,* was quickly obeyed the next morning, and we filed out of camp in good order. At this moment, our Captain, whom we had left ill at Bent's Fort, joined us; and, being deservedly a favorite, was received with hearty cheers. All the other troops preceded us through the Moro Pass; and just as a turn of the road took them from our sight, our bugler sounded the *trot.* Supposing that our comrades were already engaged, we belabored our cannon-mules into a trot with our sabres; and, in a few minutes, found the rest of the force drawn up in battle array. We galloped quickly to our position in the centre near General Kearney, who, surrounded by his staff, was standing on a small eminence. No enemy could be discovered by us; but, after half an hour's suspense, our spies came in with the intelligence that the Mexican force had fallen back on the Pecos Pass and would there entrench themselves.

We passed scattered houses and small towns, until we came to the village of Vegas, on the Gallinas river, where it passes through an immense cleft in the rocks. Here we encamped, and being on guard this night, had laid myself down about twelve o'clock to

22 • A CAMPAIGN IN NEW MEXICO

take a short nap, when I heard the sentinel near me challenge some one, who proved to be a sergeant from our outposts, with a prisoner in charge, who had been taken at one of the pickets. I accompanied the serjeant to General Kearney's tent, where we left our prisoner. The stranger was a young handsome Mexican, and declared himself to be a son of General Salazar. This young man's object was, apparently, friendly, as he stated that he had come out in order to inform us that the Mexican army, which had numbered four thousand men under the command of Governor Armijo, had been strongly intrenched at the Pecos Pass, intending to give us a warm reception, but had disbanded the night before, in consequence of some quarrel about precedence in rank among the officers; and he assured us that our entry into Santa Fé would be bloodless. Not knowing how much of this information might prove true, we took care not to lose sight of the gentleman; and an especial guard was assigned to him.

The next evening we stopped at San Miguel del Vada, where Kendall's party was so badly treated and Howland and another barbarously murdered by the same Governor Armijo. As we passed slowly through the Plaza in which these poor men had been executed, a moody silence pervaded the whole, save the whispered words "Kendall," "Alamo," "Armijo"—and everyone seemed relieved when we had left San Miguel del Vada behind us.

On the night of the 17th of August we halted at Pecos. This is a small Mexican village that takes its name from the ruins of the Indian town which formerly stood here. All that is left of what was one of the most celebrated of the Aztec towns is the church, which is of immense size, and supposed to be over five hundred years old. This is the church which contained the sacred fire, said to have been kindled by Montezuma with orders to keep it burning until his return. The fire was kept alive for more than three hundred years, when, having, by some accident, been allowed to go out and most of the town having been depopulated by disease, the remainder of the inhabitants abandoned the place and joined a

CHAPTER TWO • 23

neighboring village. There are many traditions connected with this old church, one of which is that it was built by a race of giants fifteen feet in height, but these dying off, they were succeeded by dwarfs with red heads, who, being in their turn exterminated, were followed by the Aztecs. But a singular part of the story is that both the large and the small men were white. The bones which have been dug from the floor of the church are, certainly, of gigantic size. A thigh bone that I saw could never have belonged to a man less than ten feet high. While myself and a companion were examining the edifice, a mule that we had tied outside, having got loose, very leisurely walked in after us, apparently as anxious to satisfy his curiosity as ourselves, and without hesitation went straight to the place where the altar had formerly stood. This was raised three or four steps higher than the body of the church. Up these walked the mule, and, having reached the top step, he gravely turned round and, giving vent to his feelings and piety in a long *Eehaw*, as gravely descended and walked out of the building.

The day on which we reached Santa Fé we passed through the defile in which we were to have been resisted.

On seeing the great advantages we should have had to fight against, we could only look at each other with a stare expressive of "we are well out of it." The cañon, or valley, in which the enemy were to have met us, winds between high mountains for miles and then, after passing between two enormous perpendicular rocky precipices, ascends and widens gradually for some yards. The road is on a narrow shelf of the rock, only just wide enough for a wagon, the rest of the gorge being a deep rocky gully about twenty yards across. Just at the top of the slight ascent in the road, the Mexicans, it seems, had planted their battery, having felled some trees and thrown them across the pass—thus occupying a raking position along it. The rocks on each side being too steep to climb, the only way for us would have been to carry the position by a *coup de main;* and this, well armed with artillery as they were, would have been no easy affair for us. In fact, five hundred resolute men could

24 • A Campaign in New Mexico

have defended the pass against twice our force. On the evening of the 18th day of August, we fired a salute of thirteen guns over the city of Santa Fé. Our first view of this place was very discouraging. Although much larger than any we had seen yet, still there were the same mud walls and roofs and the accompaniments of dirt, pigs and naked children. The city was, in a measure, deserted, the inhabitants having been persuaded that we should rob and ill-treat everybody and destroy everything; sobbing and crying were heard from the houses; and it was only after a long speech from our General that they were at all pacified.

The City of Santa Fé, although spread over a large extent of ground, is very thinly inhabited; and, with the exception of the buildings around the public plaza, consists only of scattered huts, surrounded by large fields of Indian corn. On one side of the public square, which is of considerable extent, stands the governor's palace. It is the only building in the whole city having glazed windows. The palace is a long mud edifice, one story high, with a portico formed by extending the roof some distance over the street, and supported by smooth trunks of trees. This portico is also extended in front of all the houses facing the plaza—and it proved a comfortable protection to our poor sentinels in rainy weather. The palace has at one end the government printing office; and at the other, the guard-house, and calaboose or prison. There are fearful stories connecting Armijo's name with this prison; and the known brutality of his disposition has undoubtedly here led him to sacrifice, for their gold, better men than himself. On examining the walls of the small rooms, I found, stuffed into holes, locks of human hair, with rude crosses drawn just above them, and invocations to the saints. I cannot exactly account for these locks of hair thus illustrated; but I observed the same thing in a wall in Santa Fé, against which, it was said, some prisoners had been shot. Around the three remaining sides of the plaza, were small shops for the accommodation of traders, who, when they arrive, immediately hire them, to show off their goods to pedlers who make

CHAPTER TWO • 25

this place their rendezvous. Indeed, it is this trade solely that gives Santa Fé its importance. These shops are not exactly such as *our* merchants at home would choose to show their goods in, being without a window—the only light that the dirty sales-room receives, is through the door. We erected, in the middle of the plaza, a high mast, from which now waves the American flag; while across the square is ranged artillery, embracing the guns we brought out, as well as the pieces we found here and elsewhere—Among the latter, is the beautiful six-pounder which Kendall's party had with them. It bears upon it the lone star of Texas, and the name of her ex-governor, "M. B. Lamar," and upon the sight is engraved "Santa Fé." Armijo, in his retreat, had buried this gun in the Pecos pass, but we found it, and had the impudence to fire our morning and evening signals from it.

Fronting the governor's palace, on the plaza, stands an old church, which was robbed of all its plate and ornaments some time before we arrived. It is allowed to go to ruin in consequence of this desecration. On each side of the altar is much fine carving, and above, there has been good painting; but the rain has beaten through the roof upon it, and nothing is now left but a head, apparently of an angel, which is beautifully painted. The date upon a tomb in the edifice is 1768, but the church itself is much older.

Although there are four other churches, there is no burying-ground, and the dead are interred by the side of the road, just out of the city, with simply a pile of stones, and a small wooden cross on the top of it. I did not witness any grown Mexican buried while I was in Santa Fé, with the exception of an officer, and he was interred with military honors; persons of both nations following to the grave. But our troops had brought the measles with them, and it was soon communicated to the children of the inhabitants, and carried off many of them; therefore, funerals among the young were common. In these processions, two men went first, bearing spades with which to dig the grave; next, music, consisting, generally, of a violin and clarionet played to some lively tune; after these

26 · A Campaign in New Mexico

came the bier, upon which was placed the body, generally without coffin—the latter, (black, with white tape crossed all over it,) being borne empty by two children across their shoulders, walking behind; the body was usually in its best clothes, strewed with flowers, and lying upon a white pall; the bier was borne on the shoulders of four children, generally girls; and after these came the friends, without any order, dressed in their most showy clothes, and most of them provided with a bottle of *aguadiente*, or home-made brandy. After the ceremonies in the church were ended, the poor little innocent was buried by the roadside, and a pile of stones raised over it; and if the father was too lazy to make a cross for his child's grave, he stole one from an adjoining stone-pile. And the funeral party went home pretty tipsy.

General Kearney occupied the governor's palace, and quarters were selected for the men, and an hospital arranged. The Mexican houses, although very uncomfortable-looking from the outside, are, generally, by no means so within, for being well whitewashed there, they look clean, and are at all times cool. The walls are built of large bricks of mud called adobes, about two feet long by one foot wide, and four inches thick; and the mud being mixed with fine cut straw, and dried in the sun, holds very well together, if carefully handled. These are built up with mud for mortar, and very often plastered with the same substance both inside and out; but, as the tools used are only a spade and wooden trowel, the walls are not generally very smooth. On the top of these walls are laid young trees, for rafters, upon which are again laid small sticks, placed close together, and, over all, a coat of mud from six to eight inches in thickness. This roof, of course, is quite flat, but the walls being built at least a foot higher than the roof on all sides, with holes here and there to let the water escape, they prevent the earth from washing off, and, as the grass soon grows upon this roof, it becomes impervious to the water. The floor is nothing but the bare earth, trodden down hard; and I can say, from experience, that it makes the hardest of beds—rock not even excepted! The walls and ceiling are whitewashed with a solution of bone-lime, made quite thick, and laid on by means of a buckskin. The houses are often whitewashed, both externally and internally, and the lime being of a brilliant white, renders the room very light, although, perhaps, the only opening is at the door, or a little grated window about a foot square—no window-glass being used. The houses of the poorer classes only consist of one room, with generally a partition wall, as high as the waist, running almost across it; and around the walls are built broad seats, upon which the blankets that compose the beds of the family are laid during the day. At night, the children use these benches as bedsteads, while the rest of the family, consisting, probably, of three generations, sleep promiscuously upon the floor, in filthy sheepskins and blankets. The better sort sleep upon sacks of feathers, and in low trundle bedsteads, hewed with an axe from the rough wood. As regards the people who inhabit the houses, it is a hard task to describe them. The children, from the age of four downwards, are generally left entirely naked—this, however, occurs more in the country than in towns. The women of Santa Fé, being mostly poor, are badly clothed, and are very dirty, which does not add to the attractiveness of their ugly dark countenances. They marry very young, but do not seem to know what virtue or modesty is; and being almost the slave of the husband, who will sit day after day in the sun, and smoke his cigaritos, without offering to assist his hard-working wife in anything, are very fond of the attentions of strangers.

Those who have much white blood in them are pretty, but these are seldom found among the lower order, which numbers as one hundred to one in proportion to the upper class.

The men are the meanest, most contemptible set of swarthy thieves and liars to be found anywhere. The rich ones will cheat and swindle; and the poor sneakingly pilfer anything. The commonest class are generally dressed in cheap dyed goat-skin pantaloons, made of two different colors, which are dressed like our buckskins and are as soft; a coarse shirt, and a blanket of a quality

28 · A CAMPAIGN IN NEW MEXICO

according to the circumstances of the wearer; a palm-leaf hat generally completes the dress. Shoes are a luxury only worn by those who can afford them, being replaced by those who cannot, with a piece of raw bullock's hide, tied on the sole of the foot. Among the better sort, the pantaloons are of cloth, ornamented with stripes of colored goatskin; and they wear blue jackets with plenty of buttons, and a black oilskin cover to their wide-brimmed hats; a hatband ornamented with silver, and a small silver plate on each side of the crown. The pantaloons of all classes have buttons all the way down the outside of each leg, which, however, are never really buttoned, but allowed to hang loose; exposing a pair of white cotton drawers under them. And more to the south, all classes wear a red sash around the waist. The part of the dress which at once tells the wealth of the wearer, is the poncho or blanket. This, although called a blanket, is nothing like the article known among us by that name, it being without nap and wove, according to value, in small or large patterns. The common ones are only white, striped with black, and worth about a dollar, and from the latter price they rise even to two hundred dollars. Some are really beautiful, and being of fine wool, show charmingly their brightly-colored small patterns. The good ones are almost impervious to rain, and you may even pour water into the folds of the poncho, and it will not run through. They are all made with a hole in the centre, through which the wearer puts his head, and as it reaches nearly to the ankles, both before and behind, it forms an excellent protection against the weather; and when not so required, it is thrown carelessly and worn, with an air, over the left shoulder. Several of the good ones, costing from fifteen to thirty dollars, were brought home for counterpanes by our men. However, this quality is only to be found on the backs of the Mexicans, and a serious obstacle presents itself to many persons against possession, for there is an universal presence of vermin on the bodies of all the inhabitants, and it is not unusual to see women and men stop suddenly, expertly hunt, and a sharp sound announces to you a death—while

Chapter Two • 29

the next minute they handle the fruit or cheese which they are offering to sell to you.

The women wear, if poor, an under garment without sleeves and one petticoat, quite short and leaving the shoulders and bosom exposed. A narrow but long scarf, either gray or black, called a reboso, is brought over the top of the head and across the face, leaving only the eyes exposed—the ends, by crossing them over the bosom, supply the place of bodice. It is under no circumstances laid aside while the owner is awake, being used dextrously even at times of working or cooking, never, however, allowed to come in the way of the occupation. The women of the higher classes are very fond of wearing an infinity of petticoats, which can all be seen one a little below another. The Mexican women are the most graceful and *boldest* walkers I know, their step being always free and good, and their carriage never too stiffly upright. From being accustomed, when young, to carry heavy jars of water on their heads, they acquire a graceful oscillation of their bodies.

The jars I mention are of all sizes; and with the rare exception of a copper pan now and then, are the only articles used to cook or hold water. They are made by the Indians out of a very abundant brick clay, being baked of a red color and glazed only inside, globular in shape, with a short neck and somewhat small mouth. At all the farms or ranchos we found the dung of cattle pressed into large slabs, which we ascertained were, when dry, to be used to bake the jars. These articles supply the place of metal vessels, as they stand heat well. Articles of metal are very scarce. I do not believe that there are two doors in all Santa Fé hung on metal hinges, they being made to turn on wooden pegs—the same with the shutters to windows.

The food of the poorer people consists of a sauce made by mixing the powdered red pepper, *Chili Colorado*, with hot water, and eaten with Tortillas. These are thin cakes, thus made: the dry Indian corn is, first, slightly parched, then ground on their mills, which consist simply of two stones; the largest, generally about

30 · A Campaign in New Mexico

two feet by one foot and a few inches thick, is hewn out of the hard boulders which abound in this country, and are cut so that, by means of two legs, they rest on the ground at an angle of 35°, while the meal is ground with the aid of the second stone, which is small and narrow, and only as long as the other stone is wide. In order to use this mill, the poor women go down on their knees, and, working the smaller stone somewhat in the manner of a painter's muller, after much trouble, manage to work the corn, with the addition of a little water, into a thick paste, which is rapidly flattened out by the woman between her hands, into thin cakes the size of a dinner-plate, and about half as thick, when it is thrown on a sheet of tin kept hot over the fire. The skill and rapidity with which the poor creatures flatten out this paste into such thin cakes are surprising—never have I seen one spoiled or broken. These tortillas are mostly of a bright sky-blue color—caused by the rind of the kernels of the maize, which is of all shades, from a bright purple to a pure white, although the dark colors predominate, and the mixture brings them to the blue. These cakes are not very inviting to a stranger; but, to the Mexicans, they supply the place of bread as well as of fork and spoon. They are very skillful with them for this purpose; and I have taken dinner with rich men when no other implement for eating was used. Another favorite dish is *Tole*, or rather *Atole*. This is prepared of various materials, mostly of the common meal. However, to make it really good, it should be prepared in an open vessel by heating a few quarts of milk or water; and when it boils, stirring in a mixture of fine wheat flour mixed with the meal of the small piñon nuts, obtained from a species of the pine tree. After being boiled a short time, it becomes very palatable, and a great satisfier of hunger. When made with only water and corn meal, it is, of course, not so inviting, although by no means bad. The meal of an ordinary Mexican man is about half a pint of red pepper, with three or four hot tortillas. This he has without variation all his life, many of them never tasting meat; while those who do, cook it only

CHAPTER TWO • 31

after it has been dried or jerked;—as we used to say, after all taste has been *jerked* out of it.

Our wood was brought to us nicely cut in short sticks by Mexicans, and packed on little donkeys. These animals are very numerous; and you may often see, moving along with a short rocking motion, large bundles of hay, fodder or other articles, without perceiving anything to cause the motion, except whisking about behind will be a donkey's tail. These animals are treated with great cruelty by their masters, who not only overload them, but, going upon the old idea that *a donkey eats nothing*, do not provide food for them. Children ride them, just jumping on and always sitting upon the hind quarters and never on the body of the animal, using a small club, with which they guide by thumping the creatures on cither side of the head. This system of guidance does very well until some green fodder or other tempting morsel meets the donkey's sight, when all the thumps and thwacks upon the head avail nothing; and a rider has no recourse but to slide down over the tail, and, by main force, push the animal away. These creatures are never harnessed in any other way than by putting on a pack saddle, and to which is fastened the equally balanced load. They are driven generally in numbers by one man on foot, who, with a short stick, thumps or pokes any loitering ass, at the same time uttering *tcsh! tcsh!* which sound comprises all the donkey vocabulary—answering for "go ahead," "stop," "turn," &c.

The Mexican mules are very poor, smaller than those of America, and are principally used for packing. Their loads vary from two hundred to four hundred pounds. The Mexicans, through carelessness, allow the mules' backs to become chafed with the pack-saddle, and they soon are useless. Occasionally a fine riding mule may be met with, commanding an exorbitant price. These poor animals, as well as the horses, often present a very ludicrous appearance, the mule, as he passes through different hands, being branded, and thus carrying his "title deeds" on his hide: each owner, on purchasing, stamps him with a hot branding iron, having a combined mark, looking most like a Spanish notary's rubric, or Chinese characters; and when he is again sold, the iron is reversed and the brand is put immediately under the former. The first is called "fierro," and the second "venta." The first place for branding is the shoulder; and as this part will hold but one brand, the neck is next used, and after that the hips and hind leg. The production of the last fierro is sure evidence of ownership; and any ignorant person, not having the "venta" branded underneath, may probably lose his mule, as the former owner can again claim the creature.

Most of the riding is upon their small mustangs or ponies, of which there is a great abundance. In the southern parts are many herds of them running wild—never having felt the control of man. While travelling southward, I suddenly came upon a herd of them; and their action, while running from me, was beautiful. One of them, in particular, a small cream-colored stallion, who seemed to be the leader, lagged a little behind; and, after taking a good look at me, galloped off, playing a thousand antics; then, after a few minutes, he would stop, and, turning his head, would have another good look—when he would again bound off. He was large for a mustang, and made me wish to have a lasso over his head. The Mexicans, when they "break in" one of these, do it thus: noosing the rope around the creature's nose, the breaker lets him bound to the extent of the rope, say from fifteen to twenty feet, when, by a skillful pull, the horse is thrown upon his back; after repeating this until the animal evidently understands that he is not free, the man gathers the rope up, and, jumping on the creature's bare back, using the rope by way of bridle, urges him on with whip, heel and voice. He goes with the speed of the wind; but becomes weary; is brought back quite subdued, and, bridled, again ridden until he is covered with foam, being completely cowed. These ponies are only used for riding, and when equipped with beautiful silver-mounted bridle and saddle, they have a pretty appearance. They are never over eleven hands high; and although well made, are not capable of great speed or possessed of much wind. They are, however, full

CHAPTER TWO • 33

of action, and can endure much thirst and hunger—thriving better on grass or fodder than on corn or oats. Generally when a Mexican mounts a horse, it is upon a very heavy silver mounted saddle, with large wooden stirrups. Behind him and upon the haunches, and entirely concealing them, there is a large flap of leather, ornamented with silver studs, or covered with long black hair. The Mexicans always arm their heels with long blunt spurs, which they keep in constant action on the ribs of the animal.

I have seen these spurs with the rowels seven inches in diameter, and the shank in proportion. All rich Mexicans carry, fastened to the pommel of the saddle, a pair of shaggy goatskins, with embroidered leather trimmings. These are used to cover the leg in hot weather, and hang from the hip to below the foot of the rider. The bit, like the spur, is of the most cruel kind—so made that it would be an easy thing to break the horse's jaw by a smart pull; and, hung inside of the mouth, are small loose pieces of copper which keep it always sore. Nothing could be better calculated than the whole equipment to ruin a horse—the sharp bit spoiling the paces, and the heavy saddle and equipments destroying his back.

CHAPTER THREE

EVERY MORNING saw collected along the southern side of the Plaza an assemblage of ugly old women, trying to sell three or four eggs, a couple of quarts of goats' milk, piñones, watermelons, or molasses made from corn stalks. When trade was dull they were actively employed upon the head of a youngster. These ancient dames also sold the dry shuck or covering of the ear of the Indian corn, cut into oblong pieces of three inches in length and one inch in width. These are for making the eternal cigarito. When neatly tied in bundles, these skins are called *hojas*. Every Mexican, male or female, carries, at the girdle, a pouch which contains a bundle of hojas and a small bottle of powdered tobacco (which is sparingly sprinkled in the shuck), and flint, steel and tinder. As tobacco is very scarce with them, they are not over free to offer a cigarito; but when they do, they always first kindle it with the assistance of the mouth. This, from their general use of garlic, does not improve the flavor of the cigarito. In the more southern provinces, the corn skin is altogether repudiated, and the paper cigarito substituted, the sale of which is a government monopoly. I did not observe a single Mexican make any other use of tobacco; and yet you rarely see either man or woman without a cigarito. Children quite small will go teasing their mothers with *"Da me una cigarita, maman?"* and, on obtaining it, they sit down quietly and smoke with the most ludicrous gravity.

The universality of the cigarito is only equaled by that of the eternal game of monte, played with cards. The suits whereof are

35

clubs, swords, suns, and cups, all delineated in their own proper colors and figures. Each suit numbers ten cards, namely, (like the American,) from ace to seven, and then knave, horse standing in the place of queen, and king. The mysteries of the game can only be learnt by losing at it. The coolness with which the Mexicans lose or win at this game is remarkable, their countenances never changing. Men and women of all degrees may be seen sitting at the green cloth covered table. It is said that the priests also indulge at it, but I never saw one playing. Sitting on the curbstones in the street, may be continually seen fellows without shoes, and almost naked, who, having scraped together a few coppers, are dealing monte, with a greasy pack of cards, for the benefit of half a dozen poor wretches as ragged as themselves. One day, in Chihuahua, I gave a little fellow, about six years of age, a quartilla, a small copper coin worth three cents. The child went up to its mother, and holding up the coin, lisped out "monte." His gaming propensities seemed to have come upon him as early as his *Da me una cigarita, maman.*

Although Gregg, in his work on the Commerce of the Prairies, speaks of the valley of Santa Fé as a fine grazing spot, we found it just the contrary, there not being any grass within twenty miles; and we were obliged to send our horses as far as Galisteo to find a sufficiency. After a time, we sent them to Bent's Farm, above Taos, where there is always grazing to be had all the year round. The only objection is the distance, being over a hundred miles.

On the second of September, General Kearney, having first appointed George Bent, Esquire, civil governor of New Mexico, started on a reconnaissance down the Rio Grande, with five hundred of Colonel Doniphan's regiment, one hundred and fifty artillery, (the writer being among them,) and one hundred regulars, leaving the remainder of the troops to garrison Santa Fé.

Our first encampment was at the village of San Domingo, which is inhabited by the Puebla Indians, and supplies Santa Fé with the small amount of fruit which it consumes. It has a very pretty appearance, every house being surrounded by small fruit trees. We

CHAPTER THREE · 37

were received here in Indian style. The inhabitants were dressed in the gayest trappings; all mounted and armed. They dashed down towards us at full speed, and only when almost touching us, wheeled to right and left along our front, all the while discharging their few guns and pistols; and after separating into two parties, and going through a mimic battle, they formed around our officers, and escorted them into the place. These were the largest and finest Indians I saw, and were dressed in showy costume. I observed one particularly. It was a coat, or rather shirt of bright blue and red cloth, half of each color; the division running down the chest and back—the coat, as well as the buckskin leggins, being trimmed with blue and white beads very handsomely. Although they evidently liked to be noticed, yet they did not move a muscle of their painted faces, as we handled their dresses. They behaved hospitably; and were evidently satisfied with the change that had taken place in the government.

The next place worth mentioning is Albuquerque, a town of some size. It has a fine church (although made of mud). The residence of ex-governor Armijo is here. His wife was in the town, at his residence, which has since been used as barracks for a detachment of our troops.

The priest's house, which I saw the inside of while on another visit to Albuquerque, is the best *adobe* dwelling I observed in the country. The priests are high in position, and always rich; but in morals and character they are, with few exceptions, even below their followers. It is not unusual for them to have three or four wives, all living in the house with them, who, as well as the other people, manifest the most servile attention to them. It really used to make my blood boil, to see these poor wretches come into the room where I might happen to be in conversation with the padre, and after kneeling down and kissing the hem of his garment, stand on one side, hat in hand, awaiting the moment when he might condescend to speak to them; while the rascal was trying, with all his skill, to cheat me in the bargain I was making with him; not

38 · A Campaign in New Mexico

scrupling to tell the most abominable falsehoods, if they became necessary to aid his plan. Even in the street, the people will frequently kneel and kiss his robe, as he passes them, while he manifests, outwardly, no knowledge of the salute, passing on as if he had attracted no notice.

Until we reached Tomae, which was to be the extent of our journey, we passed no place worth mentioning except Valentia, which is a large and handsome town, supported by its extensive vineyards, which add to the appearance of the place, being interspersed with melon patches and fruit trees. The vines are neither staked nor trellised, but grow to the height of perhaps four feet, perfectly straight, and when at that height spread out broad and bushy. The grapes are very fine, and of the Muscatel kind.

At this town, many of the soldiers being almost destitute of money—none of the troops having received any pay—stripped their coats of their military buttons, and passed them for the value of twelve and a half cents each—buying fruit with them.

The most industrious part of the population is Indian; and many came to our camp with fruit. The Indians are well made, but seldom over five feet in height. They are dressed in tunics of the same material as the Mexican blanket, and wear what is called the Navajo poncho; so named from being made by the Navajo Indians. It is of very fine texture, with both sides alike, and the pattern always in broad black and white stripes.

The women are singular objects; not over four feet in stature, with little round faces, of a rich light copper color. Their dress consists of a tunic of blue or white, made quite full, with a girdle at the waist, and being made very low at the neck, without sleeves, only descend to the knees; while the leg, from the knee downwards, is wrapped closely in several finely dressed goatskins, which end in a neat moccason—all this giving them a singular yet pretty appearance. The hair is cut short all round the head, and kept nicely trimmed.

Drawn together by the upper two corners, and around their neck, they wear what is called a "tilma." It is a beautiful robe, about

CHAPTER THREE • 39

three feet square, woven of black mules' hair, with a showy edging of red. One of these little women, with a basket of grapes or peaches placed upon her head, which apparently pressed her broad good-humored face into a yet more good-humored expression, and accompanied by three or four naked children, made a picturesque object.

We arrived at Tomae on the eve of a great religious fete. The celebration of which commenced over night, by the firing of guns, and the ringing of bells, and this was continued all through the following day. I would warn a lover of campanology against Mexican bell ringing, for nine out of ten of their bells are cracked, and the study is to make the greatest possible noise. During the morning, mass was celebrated; and the figure of the Virgin Mary was carried along the streets in procession—in which walked General Kearney and his officers with lighted candles in their hands. The day closed with very tolerable fireworks, which, however, were got up on the same principle as the bell ringing, viz., to make the utmost noise.

There were also several fandangos in town. The word fandango is only used when you wish to express a ball among the peasantry; and much fun is to be found at them. The largest rooms are of course selected. At one end, carpets are spread, and all the women squat themselves on them, the men occupying the remainder of the room. The most common dance is the *cuna*, which resembles our Spanish dance. After all the couples are placed, the women begin a song, as dreary and monotonous as a dead march. The song keeps time with two squeaking fiddles. After each dance, your partner is allowed to find her way to her seat alone, where she again squats herself down, unless you have invited her to take a glass of brandy or wine—a stall for the sale of which is always kept in an adjoining room—and where, also, is generally kept a monte table.

At a ball, *baille* of the higher class, the singing would, of course, be vulgar, but generally there are the squatting, fiddling, inviting and monte table.

40 • A Campaign in New Mexico

On our return from Tomae, all the troops were quartered in the houses formerly occupied by the soldiers of Armijo. It would have been better for us if we had remained in camp, for the accommodations were not spacious, and bilious fever began to carry off the men. The stock of medicines was reduced so low as to become alarming. In order to show the limited size of our quarters, the room that I and eight others were in was only about fourteen feet by eight. Here we cooked, ate and slept; and had, as it may well be presumed, close stowage at night. It was lighted by a window hole about fifteen inches square. Most of my company, however, had their health. We seem to have been an exception to the general sickliness. A gentleman recently from Santa Fé tells me there are now over three hundred graves of American soldiers in the burying-ground under the walls of Fort Marcy. This fort is on the top of a very high hill, commanding the town and surrounding country. It was built by the troops who remained in Santa Fé during the winter, and the cold work was frequently put a stop to by the snow.

During the latter part of September, a detachment of fifty men from the artillery companies, under the command of Captain Fisher, was sent towards the North, in order to bring in some of the chiefs of the Apache tribe of Indians, with a view to force them into a treaty, as they had been committing depredations on the Mexicans. After three days' scrambling over steep mountains, up and down which our horses had to be led, and after passing through numerous villages, we met several of the chiefs upon the road. They at once consented to return with us. These men were very commanding in their appearance, of a remarkably large size, and having a wild look. I was amused with an old chief who appeared to be the oracle. As we had invited these Indians to come with us, of course we had to feed them. We gave them some flour and bacon. They boiled the bacon and then stirred the flour into the same water. The former of these rather puzzled them, particularly the rind, which resisted their knives. As they did not understand it, they appealed to the old chief, who gravely declared, after

CHAPTER THREE • 41

much examination, that it was bone with which the American pigs were encased—all my assurances to the contrary notwithstanding. The old chief's two sons were with him, and one of them was the possessor of a beautiful elk-horn bow, which I coveted very much. We amused ourselves by getting them to shoot at pieces of tobacco. These pieces were about the size of a sixpence and were placed at one end of a fallen tree, while they would sit upon the other end, and, after removing the iron points of their arrows, they would shoot, and seldom miss striking the prize.

Our journey had ended just by the village of San Ildefonso, and we encamped in the plaza of that village. Here I witnessed the fabrication of sugar from corn stalks. The alcalde owns the mill and boiling house, and the using of these is paid in syrup. The owner of the corn stalks assembles his neighbors, and, proceeding to the mill, places the stalks, cut into short pieces, in a large wooden trough; and each man, arming himself with a heavy mallet, soon breaks the stalks into small fragments. Boiling water is poured upon them, and then the mass is put into a hollow tree set upright in a trough; into this a plug is loosely fitted, across which a long pole fixed at one end is laid, and all the young people getting upon this lever, the juice is soon pressed out and poured into earthen pots built into the top of a large furnace kept burning night and day; women continually stirring the liquor, until it is thick, when it is run into small clay moulds (unless it should be wanted for molasses). The workmen are repaid by an invitation to the house of the owner of the sugar, where they are regaled with molasses and tortillas. In this way these people help each other through the busiest seasons. They were, also, getting in their wheat while we were there. After being reaped and bound into sheaves, it is spread over a clay threshing floor, in the open air, and surrounded by high poles. Upon it are men with rude pitchforks, made of limbs of small trees. They throw the straw into the air as oxen, driven round the enclosure, trample out the grain. The poles keep in the large straw and let the light part blow away. The straw, by this means, is broken up very fine, but being of no use to them, is not regarded. The wheat, after being collected, is carefully washed by the women and children, and then spread upon cloths to dry. The agricultural implements are very rude. Their ploughs are made of wood, without a particle of iron, and very often in one piece, which is in the shape of a three pointed star, with one of the points short, and to one of the longer ends is attached, by means of a raw-hide-rope, oxen yoked by binding a long stick to their horns; the other long end serves for a handle, while the short one turns up the ground. A rude heavy hoe and a common spade are precious things.

On our return, we passed through a large town, inhabited by the Puebla Indians, called Tezuque. Here I first saw the singular custom which these Indians have of making the entrance to their houses by a ladder placed against the second story window, there being no opening to the lower story. This makes each house an easily defended place, for the raising the ladder leaves no easy ingress. The village looked pretty—numerous bowers of green branches being erected outside the place to protect the women and children from the sun, while making the earthen jars I have previously mentioned.

The Indians we brought in very willingly came to terms. They saw they had men of a different character from Mexicans to deal with. As to the latter, although perhaps armed with carbine and sabre, twenty would frequently fly before a couple of Indians. But here were only fifty of us marching to subdue, if necessary, their village of, probably, two thousand inhabitants. Our Indians moved on—those who had wives taking them with them upon their mules, while others, who had not, going on foot and outwalking our best horses, and, no doubt, all thinking to receive handsome presents. These people are powerful and brave, but treacherous. A year or two before we had arrived in Santa Fé, they were invited into the city by Governor Armijo, and signed a treaty and received presents. On departing, they took the opportunity to stop in the outskirts, murder several herdsmen, and drive off a large quantity of cattle.

CHAPTER THREE • 43

Before proceeding on the southern trip to Tomae, I witnessed one of the ridiculous mummeries frequently practised by the priests. Our men, while at the grazing camp at Galisteo, were kept two days accidentally without their regular supplies of food; and, therefore, were obliged to forage upon the corn-fields around, especially as the inhabitants had previously refused to sell any to us; and it had also been our constant habit to boil a pot of maize each night just before going to sleep, and, sitting round the fire, to eat and talk. The surrounding corn-fields began to look rather unproductive, much to the astonishment of the natives; so, to remedy this, the figure of the Virgin Mary was carried around the fields, in solemn procession—solemn, perhaps, to the poor Mexicans, but by no means so to us. The figure, which was very fantastically dressed, was carried by a woman in the same manner as she would have carried a child, and over them was held an old red umbrella, the only one in the village, and reserved for great occasions like the present. At the head of the procession walked the priest, book in hand, sprinkling holy water on all sides, followed by two musicians with squeaking fiddles, and also by two men firing off continually a couple of old rusty fowling pieces, to the great admiration of the young folks. After them came the figure; and the procession was closed by all the rest of the inhabitants. At every twenty or thirty steps they would all kneel down and pray audibly. We smoothed our faces as we best could, not wishing to be supposed to know anything about the maize just then.

During the early part of the month of October (1846) Colonel Price's regiment from Missouri arrived at Santa Fé; and General Kearney having left for California with all the regulars, Colonel Doniphan immediately withdrew his regiment from the place and left Colonel Price in command, marching southward, with a view, first, to bring the Navajo Indians to terms, and then proceed, as he supposed, to report himself to General Wool, who was expected to be near or in possession of the city of Chihuahua.

44 • A Campaign in New Mexico

Soon after Colonel Price's arrival, the Mormons, numbering five hundred, with several women and children, arrived, on their way to California; and on the 12th of September an express—on its way to Washington—brought intelligence of Colonel Fremont's success in that country. This intelligence induced General Kearney to send back nearly half of his men, some of whom were posted at Albuquerque, while the remainder were sent to Fort Leavenworth, with the horses of the whole force—they having previously been mounted upon mules. We were sorry to part with General Kearney. He had gained the good wishes of every man; and I believe that the Taos insurrection and the murder of Governor Bent and others would not have taken place if he had remained.

During the month of November a dramatic society was started by several members of our battalion, patronized by all the officers, and upon mentioning the want of a suitable room to Governor Bent, he immediately gave us the use of the large fandango room in the palace, which we soon converted into a handsome theatre. A good wardrobe and suitable scenery were procured with great difficulty, but in the middle of the month we opened with Pizarro and Bombastes Furioso. From this time until the first of December, when most of the performers went South, we played to crowded houses. Our greatest difficulty was on the score of female performers, being obliged to take these from the ranks; but, luckily, three of the society made very good looking women when dressed in character. The Mexican ladies would persist in smoking during the whole performance, and they generally laughed where they ought to have cried, and *au contraire*, but, on the whole, were much pleased.

Towards the latter end of November an order was published by command of Colonel Price that ten men from each company of his own regiment, as well as from the artillery companies, should be selected by their respective captains, "with regard to their mental as well as their physical capabilities," to be well mounted and to form an escort of one hundred men to accompany Lieut.-Colonel D. D. Mitchell in an effort to open a communication with General

Wool, who was supposed, as I have before remarked, to be in or near Chihuahua. The writer had the honor to be appointed Assistant to the Quartermaster of this escort, or, as it is termed, Quartermaster-Sergeant. At first, Captain Weightman was named as the officer selected to command our little force, and this made every man eager to go, being sure of good treatment. However, Captain Hudson, who was not a favorite, was appointed, and we started with only ninety-five men, in consequence.

On the 1st of December (1846) I bade farewell to Santa Fé, and I trust I may never again see its dirty, unpaved streets. In a few days we arrived at Albuquerque. Here we crossed the Rio Grande, which was only waist deep. The weather had been very cold before we left Santa Fé; but still most of us slept outside of our tents. One morning, on waking, I raised my head, which caused a quantity of snow that had fallen during the night to get into my neck, giving me a sudden cold bath. On looking about, I could only see the rounded forms of my companions lying under the snow. After passing the Rio Grande, we travelled down its opposite bank, which was thickly settled both by Indians and Mexicans.

While on our journeys southward we had to buy corn, wood and fodder every night. This duty, generally, fell to my lot, and although we had an interpreter, I soon managed to pick up enough Spanish to purchase without his assistance. At one of the Indian towns called Iseleta, I found a regular monastery; and making inquiries where I could buy corn, a jolly looking old monk in a cowl and rope told me he would be too happy to accommodate me. After partaking of a bottle of good wine with him, he took me to an upper room in one of the corners of the church, and showed me a large quantity of Indian corn piled up, being the tithes from the poor inhabitants. After purchasing a sufficiency, which was measured in sacks, two of which are supposed to hold, when the corn is shelled out, a *fanega*, equal to two bushels and a quarter, I found the padre was trying hard to cheat me, both in measure and count; so, taking an opportunity to *accidentally* put out the light, I told

46 · A Campaign in New Mexico

the ten men who were with me to fill up their sacks, which were larger than the measuring sack, and also not to forget their pockets. When the light returned, every man had his full sack on his shoulder ready to carry off. The old fellow, evidently, noticed the fullness of the sacks, but knew it was not worth while to say anything—so, after all, he did not make much out of me.

The Mexican measures are less than ours; for instance, their leagues are only about two and a half miles; a yard is thirty inches; the pint and the quart are proportionably undersized. South of Chihuahua things are sold by the arroba of 25 pounds weight: thus, if you want to buy 100 pounds of flour you ask for four arrobas. Their Fanega, which is used to measure grain, contains, in New Mexico, 2½ bushels, and further south 2¼, which is divided into 12 measures called Almos. The Fanega measure is in the shape of the box of a wheelbarrow, that is, oblong, but with one end at an angle, and open at the top and branded by the government at all the joints.

At Sabinal I had again to deal with a priest; and upon presenting myself at his house, I found him a little dried up young man, and from the first, did not like the look of his countenance. He was in his small store, in which he sold "odd notions," and among them native whisky. After bargaining with him for a quantity of corn, which he charged for at the rate of about two dollars and a half the bushel, I observed in his court yard two black sheep, which he told me he was fattening up for his own eating, but I soon bought them at a dollar a piece. The only difficulty was in catching them. I was, from laughter, soon incapable of assisting in this. The priest, who had his long silk gown on, whisked it under his arm, and running at the sheep, attempted several times to catch them; but one would bolt between his legs, knocking him down, while the other jumped over his head. But he was not discouraged, particularly as I made it a part of the bargain that they were to be delivered. At last, on one of them jumping over the priest, he caught it by the hind legs and came to me triumphant. I never saw a more ridiculous figure than his reverence with the sheep struggling on his back. In the evening, while measuring the corn, a dispute about it arose between us, he trying to cheat me. At last he told me that I lied! On which, I caught him by the neckcloth, drew out my butcher's knife, told him that, in my opinion, he was a rascal, and that if he dared to repeat such words, I should use my cold steel. This brought him to his senses at once, the people, who had just before been kissing his hands and garments, stared at me as if I were a wild beast, although I could see that some were secretly well pleased at the strong hints I gave the Padre. Upon leaving the house, I read him a short sermon on the impropriety of insulting Americans, and this had such an effect on him, that he presented me with a glass of excellent brandy as a peace-offering, which I *generously* accepted.

On the day before we arrived at the ruins of Valverde, where we were again to cross the river, a trifling occurrence took place. My duty consisted partly in seeing that the wagon-train, which was frequently five or six miles behind, got safely into camp. In order to protect the train, I had a wagon-guard of twelve men; and among them, was a tall, lanky Missourian, standing nearly seven feet high, and of almost inconceivable thinness, whose *sobriquet* was Lightning Rod. The last of our wagons having been detained this day, some distance behind the others, I remained with it, having among them my long friend. After travelling with it until about five o'clock in the afternoon, I observed a smoke ascending from a wood, about two miles off the road, to the left; and I sent Lightning Rod to see if it was our camp. I observed that he did not enter the timbered part, and only gave a look into it from a short convenient distance. When he returned he told me, in rather a troubled tone, that it was not our encampment, and that he could not imagine what it was, as he saw immense herds of cattle and numerous tents more than twenty feet in length. This of course convinced me that it was not our camp, but also excited much speculation among us, as to whose it could be, and the size of the tents especially puzzled us. I continued along the road for three or four miles, when a

Mexican, whom I met, assured me that it *was* our company. More and more surprised, I turned back, when, upon approaching the camp so wonderfully described by Lightning-rod, I found it to be the one I was in search of—his suspicious fear having multiplied five beef cattle into a herd, and our four wagons into numerous tents twenty feet in length. It was some time before he heard the last of that adventure.

After again crossing the Rio Grande at Valverde, once a fine place, but now destroyed by the Navajos, where the water was hardly as deep as we had found it at Albuquerque, we came upon Colonel Doniphan, encamped on the river bank, with only about eighty men. He had dispatched Major Gilpin ahead with one battalion of about four hundred. He, himself, was only waiting to collect the remainder of his command, which was scatted through the mountains, on an expedition against some Navajo Indians, who had murdered two of his men while tending a quantity of sheep. However, the Colonel at once made up his mind to accompany us with what men he now had, amounting to about fifty; and the next morning we started, expecting to be joined by straggling parties as we proceeded.

My readers may like to have a slight sketch of Colonel Doniphan. In age, about forty; and in stature, six feet two inches; of large frame; and with a very intelligent face. His great charm lies in his easy and kind manner. On the march he could not be distinguished from the other soldiers, either by dress, or from his conversation. He ranked high as a lawyer in Missouri. The colonel is in the habit of interlarding his language with strong expressions which many eastern men would call something very like swearing.

At Fray Christobal we encamped one day to cook for the two following, as, during this time, we were to be away from water—being about to cross the large bend which the river here takes. This dry stretch of road is called *La Jornada del Muerto*, or The (day's) Journey of Death. Although the word *Jornada* only means a day's journey, yet, from this day forward, our men called every

Chapter Three • 49

long dry extend of road a Jornada. In passing through the country, if you ask a peasant how far it is from one place to another, he will tell you so many jornadas (pronounced hornarthars), meaning, that to encamp at water each night, it will take so many days to travel it. But, as they always estimate road by the time it takes a pack-mule to go over it, you must allow accordingly. This long piece of road, La Jornada del Muerto, obtained its name from the circumstance of a Mexican having attempted to cross it in a day, and from his not being provided with water or food, having perished on the road. It is usually called ninety, but, by the road we followed, it is really not more than sixty miles in length. Near to the middle of it is a large hollow in the ground, which, if rain has fallen lately, usually contains water. A Spaniard who had just come through informed us that this was dry.

About noon on the following day, we entered upon this dreary journey; and after travelling fifteen miles, sent all of our live stock six miles off the road for water, to where there was a small spring. I took my horse, old Tom, to it, but was sorry, afterwards, I did so, as the long distance, twelve miles there and back, had wearied more than the water had refreshed him.

We again moved on, and marched until twelve o'clock at night; and pushed forward after daybreak.

One thing we particularly observed: that here the grass was finer and better than we had ever seen elsewhere, which, from the want of water and scarcity of rain, was a singularity.

We first met, on this part of the road, with the species of palm called by us soap-weed, from the fact that the Mexicans use its root as a substitute for soap, for which it answers very well. Indeed, it is considered superior to it for the washing of woollens. I believe it is rightly named the Lechuguilla.

This singular shrub, which is, to be also met with on the prairies, but where it never grows to any considerable size, consists of a trunk very pithy, surmounted by a fine head of stiff leaves, each of which is about two feet and a half in length, and armed at the end with a long thorn. The leaves project from the stalk on all sides, and set as close as possible, and are of a dark-green color. The flower is white and very pretty. As each year's foliage decays, it drops down against the trunk of a light-brown color. These dry leaves, when fire is applied, flash up like gunpowder, and burn with a bright light. Our night marches could be marked by their flames, which, as the nights were cold (although the days were comfortable) were cheering.

I have been thus particular in describing this plant for several reasons: one is, its many uses—of the leaves, the natives make their hats; also, when dressed like hemp, it is formed into ropes and sacks, looking like the material known as Manilla-hemp, though coarser. These plants have a singularly provoking quality; being from two to eight feet in height, they will assume to the eye, in the twilight, the most deceptive forms. To the sentinel, they will appear as forms of men; and many an unconscious soap-weed has run the chance of a sentry's shot, from not answering to the challenge of "Who goes there?" If your mule or horse has strayed from camp, and you start to hunt for him in the gray of the morning, you are sure to be led first in one direction and then in another, by one of these shrubs, which, from a short distance, has taken the form of your animal. Time after time you may have been thus deceived—yet never seeming to learn experience from a soap-weed.

Some of our men, thinking to avoid the usual suffering for water on this trip, got rather tipsy just before entering the jornada, calculating that, with a canteen full of whisky, they could keep in that state all the way across. Some did so, but others having used their canteens too freely, exhausted their stock the first night, and suffered terribly from thirst.

The second night, about eleven o'clock, we again struck the Rio del Norte, having left the old road and moved to the right to reach it. Here we found the traders, who had left Santa Fé in September, encamped with their wagons, being too much alarmed to continue their journey. The night before we arrived, one of them

CHAPTER THREE • 51

had hitched up his teams to start back to Santa Fé, some friendly Mexicans having brought intelligence from El Paso, that the priest there, named Ortis, was raising a party of men to come and rob them. Our arrival put an end to their alarm. Encamped here and a few miles below were about three hundred wagons belonging to the traders; and to one who has never seen these travelling merchants on their journey, the whole is interesting. Their wagons, called Conestoga or Pennsylvanian, are of the largest kind, covered with three or four cotton covers or sheets drawn close at each end so as to exclude moisture, and these are supported by high hoops, and, as those at the ends of the wagon are much higher than those in the middle, it has a very singular appearance. The height to the top of these end-hoops is usually from eighteen to twenty feet. They are each drawn by ten mules or six yoke of oxen, and contain about forty hundred weight of goods each. Seen from a distance, while moving on their way—one following another, with their long strings of mules, always harnessed, with the smallest in the lead, and gradually increasing in size to those at the pole or tong, upon the left one of which the driver sits with his long whip in one hand, and single rein in the other, with the sun shining on the white covers,—they present a very interesting sight.

On the twenty-third of December we encamped just below the new and rich town of Doña Ana, where we found Major Gilpin and his battalion who had preceded us. He gave as his opinion that we should have trouble in entering El Paso, but being a sanguine officer, we knew not how far to be guided by it.

That night, our picket-guard took a Scotchman, who was lurking around the camp. He was ragged and footsore; and said he had escaped from the Calaboose in El Paso, and was starving. Food was given to him, but it was remarked that he did not very well support the character of starvation—not paying much attention to our humble fare. From subsequent events, I have no doubt he was a spy from the Mexicans.

52 · A Campaign in New Mexico

The next day (the twenty-fourth), we encamped in a wood which we named Dead Man's Grove, from the circumstance of our finding, among the bushes near to our camp, three unburied bodies; and from their dresses, two must have been Americans and the third a Spaniard. Who they were or how they came there has remained a mystery—the probability is that they were murdered by Mexican scouts.

This evening, I killed fifteen sheep for our company, which had been procured on our route above. Although apparently healthy and three years old, they, when dressed, weighed only seventeen pounds on an average; some, it is true, twenty-five pounds, but others not more than twelve. I could not have believed the want of substance, if I had not weighed them myself. (A New York sheep will weigh over forty pounds.) Our mess, this night, illuminated the carcase which had been served out to them by enclosing a lighted candle in it, and its thinness made a capital lantern; some suggested that such fine mutton should have been reserved for the following day, to help out a Christmas dinner—little knowing the sort of celebration which was in store!

CHAPTER FOUR

SUNDAY, Christmas Day. We moved on; and as my place was behind with the wagons, I generally got into the camp some time after the others. However, this afternoon, I had preceded my wagons about a mile, accompanied by two of the wagon-guard. On rounding a turn of the road, I observed our little army encamping some distance ahead; and also, a mile further on, I had, for some time, noticed an immense cloud of dust which, until this moment, I had supposed to have been caused by our own men. A moment after and there were evidently great hurry and bustle in camp. Men at a distance were throwing down the wood they were bringing in, and hurrying to their arms. A man upon a white mule came dashing back at full speed, telling me to hasten up the wagons, for the enemy were upon us, and continued his headlong career, never stopping until he got safely to the rear guard six miles behind. Never was a body of men taken more by surprise. When the dust was first observed, there were not one hundred and fifty men in camp, the rest being scattered after wood and water. But all seemed to have found out the cause of the rising dust at the same moment, and came in, in double quick time, to get their arms. I immediately galloped up to the surgeon and requested orders. He told me to draw up the wagons into a close circle, or, as we called it, to *corraal* them. I quickly did so, sending to hurry on the ox-teams, which were several miles behind. By the time I had got twenty wagons in form, a man came furiously for cartridges. The wagons of Colonel Doniphan's men, which con-

53

tained their ammunition, were not yet up; but, knowing that in one of mine there were two boxes of rifle and carbine ammunition, I immediately jumped upon it and commenced throwing off the tents and things which covered the cases. As this wagon stood in what may be considered the front of the half circle I had formed, I could not help stealing a glance now and then towards the camp, where I observed our men drawn up on foot, in single line, across the road; and the Mexicans appearing in a line parallel to them. Just at the top of a slight rise in the ground, the latter drew up in good order, with the cavalry on our left and a small howitzer in the center—their left flank and body being composed of infantry—and gay enough they looked, their cavalry in bright scarlet coats with bell buttons, and snow-white belts, carrying polished sabres and carbines and long lances, with red and green pennons, while their heads were protected by brass helmets with large black plumes. The Mexicans halted—and from their ranks came a lieutenant, in handsome uniform, waving a black flag, having a skull and cross bones worked upon it. Our interpreter advanced to meet him. The lieutenant informed him that the Mexican General wished his General to come and have a parley with him. He answered him to the effect that "he wished he might get him!" Whereupon the Mexican, turning back, exclaimed, "Then prepare for a charge: we give and take no quarter!" When he reached his lines, they immediately opened their fire upon us—steadily advancing. A few minutes afterwards they fired another volley. I was still on the wagon. These two volleys of the Mexicans, though mostly fired too high to injure our troops, nevertheless rained their balls with their sharp *whist!* sound, too thick among *us* at the wagons to be pleasant; and one of them, I afterwards found, had passed through a fold in my shirt just below the left arm.

Our men, all this time, had not fired a shot.

Just in the rear of our line, and, therefore, between it and the *Corraal*, were just about fifteen of our horsemen, who had come up just at the moment, not one of the others having had time to saddle-up.

CHAPTER FOUR • 55

Again the Mexicans poured in a heavy fire, at pistol shot, wounding several men. Just as the smoke of this discharge lifted, two powerful volleys were poured in by our men from their rifles, while, at the same moment, the Mexican dragoons charged gallantly down on our left flank; but, being turned by the heavy shower of balls, swerved to their right, and, coming round the end of our line, they dashed down on the circle of wagons. Here, I had received orders to take charge; and found myself the commander of from fifteen to twenty men. I directed them to keep out of sight until the redcoats were within ten yards of us—then, we each stepped out and gave them our fire. This caused them again to swerve, and to disappear over a rising ground, whither they were hotly pursued by our little band of fifteen horsemen.

During this time, a part of our men, who were in front of the Mexican cannon, ran up, and forcibly secured and dragged it down to our ranks. This was a daring act, almost ridiculous from its fearlessness.—The idea of about thirty soldiers taking it into their heads, for they had no orders to break line, to make such a charge on the enemy's artillery! Some of our men got as many as half a dozen shots at Mexicans; but most of the latter had such pressing business somewhere else, that it was difficult, after two volleys, to get a fair sight at them.

Just as the Mexicans were about to fire their first round, our right wing received orders to kneel, which they did, and so remained until they, themselves, fired. They all rose at once to do so. The Mexicans said, afterwards, they could not understand such a people, for, not only did they sustain three volleys without returning one, which, of itself, was very puzzling, but, when one row was mowed down, up sprang another out of the grass. Most of the wounded were brought to the wagons, where we had made preparations to receive them, by spreading tents and other covering over the ground.

A fine-looking Mexican boy was brought in badly wounded. He was about fifteen or sixteen years of age, and said he had been forced to fight against us, although his heart was for us; and his mother and brother had advised him to join us as soon as possible, and this he had intended to do. Poor lad! That night, in his agony, he

56 • A Campaign in New Mexico

crawled a little away from the tent he had been laid in, and expired. We all felt interested in him, and many had visited him. Most of his talk was of his mother and sisters, and his friends, the Americans. We knew he could not recover, and yet we had not the heart to tell him so.

One of the wounded brought in, was a fine-looking sergeant of the Mexican dragoons. I believe he was the man who had headed the charge. The poor fellow had three balls through his belly, from side to side, and two horrible sabre cuts upon his head. He could not make out why he was brought in so carefully, and a place made for him to lie down on. I assured him he should be well treated; but his looks showed his incredulity. I never shall forget the tremulous grasp of the hand he gave me, when I received him under my charge. I brought the doctor to him, who, after examining him, told me there was no hope, but that if he was alive in the morning he would dress his wounds. Yet this man recovered, and was released before we left El Paso.

A little German amongst us, called after one of Dumas' three mousquetaires, Grimaud, attracted our attention. At the second volley, a ball entered the front of his cap, and raked the top of his skull, and, though only cutting the scalp, caused a great effusion of blood, which ran down his face. For a moment he thought himself mortally wounded; but, still, catching up his carbine, he fired away, crying out "Well! I'll have a crack before I die, any how." Grimaud was a favorite, and his frightfully bloody face and reckless action must be long remembered by many of us.

I did all I could to make the wounded prisoners comfortable and easy, having stationed for them a protective guard. Just after the contest had ended, a tall, barefooted Missourian came stalking to the wagons, crying out, "Where are those yellow-skinned devils? They came upon me so quickly, that I had to go at them barefoot; and while I was away, some rascal hooked my shoes. So, if there's a pair among the prisoners I'll have them."

Our number in this engagement was not over five hundred, while the Mexicans had twelve hundred men. We had but seven wounded—none killed. How we came off so well I cannot make

CHAPTER FOUR • 57

out, or the bullets rained about the troops. The Mexican loss in killed and wounded was about two hundred men.*

Among the spoils, were several kegs of wine of the best quality, which were passed from hand to hand until they were empty; and also some very nice and fine bread. There was plenty of ammunition, and also several cases of surgical instruments. The field was strewed with bodies of men and horses, lances, swords, helmets, trumpets, carbines and other war emblems.

It was rumored that there were two Mexican women in the action serving at the cannon; and that a rifle ball striking one of them in the forehead, the other bore her off the field. I do not doubt it. The women have much more courage and even sense than the men.

I afterwards heard that when the remainder of the Mexican troops reached El Paso, which they did very expeditiously, they reported that they had been defeated entirely by our infantry; and that our cavalry had not come up, but was rapidly approaching. It was some time before I could understand this matter, for we had no reserve—all our men being in the action. But the key of the affair was equal to something of Sister Anne's in Blue Beard;—we had two thousand sheep in the rear of our baggage train, and the dust raised by them had been taken for the signs of horsemen approaching. The dragoons, who had charged us so gallantly, met with the worst usage; for our little squadron of horse having chased them into the mountains, a band of Navajo Indians, who had been watching the struggle from their concealment, set upon them and killed almost all for the sake of their bright uniform and arms.

And thus ended the first battle fought by the army of the West; and called BRACITO from the bend of the river, near where we fought, which bears this name.**

Before we left the battle-ground, we dug a large hole and buried those who had fallen on the field and those who had died

---

*See the official report of the battle in the Appendix, No. 1.

**On maps of this country, many names will be found where, in truth, there is not a house. This is because the places are regular camping-grounds for caravans.

during the night; but I have understood since that wolves scratched up the bodies, and that the remnants of uniforms were now scattered over the ground.

We fully expected to have another skirmish before entering the city of El Paso, and were, therefore, on the alert. On the evening of the 26th of December we encamped at a salt pond, a short distance from the place; and twice that night were aroused by alarms, and stood for some time ready in ranks—but nothing occurred.

The next day, while on the march, we were met by several citizens of El Paso, bearing a white flag, who, at once, surrendered the place to Colonel Doniphan, and, towards evening, we entered this beautiful city. The inhabitants had mostly fled; but they all returned before we left. Those who had remained came creeping cautiously out of their houses, with baskets of fruit, which they kindly forced the soldiers to accept. By the time I reached the Plaza, I had both holsters and pockets filled.

This place (which receives its name, not, as has been frequently stated, from a pass of the river between the mountains, but from the circumstance of refugees from Santa Fé, in 1680, having here crossed the river and founded a town), is now upwards of six miles in length and from half a mile to a mile wide. It is surrounded by extensive vineyards. The mode of cultivating the grape is the same as I have mentioned to be practised at Valentia.

The valley here is the best calculated for the cultivation of the vine of any part of Mexico, the soil not being too rich, and, although there may be now and then a sharp frost, no snow has fallen there for years. At the time we arrived, December, of course there was no foliage to be seen; but I can well imagine how beautiful must be this valley when all the vines and fruit trees are in leaf and bloom.

The city and gardens are watered by numerous *sakos* or ditches supplied by the river which is dammed up just above. By means of these, the husbandmen are able to dispense with the aid of rain, which is scarce at all times in New Mexico. Each field is provided with a small running ditch; and, by cutting the bank, the water soon floods the ground. Each farmer has a day allowed him to use the water in this way, but cannot touch it at other times without the permission of the special alcalde of sakos, or, as we should term him, perhaps, commissioner of the water-works. This officer has the powers of a judge in all things relating to his department. Every person is required to keep his sako in repair; and should any damage occur to his neighbor's property by inattention, the delinquent has to make good the damage. One poor fellow told me that, in consequence of the frost, the side of his sako had given way during the night, and had injured a quantity of wine in his neighbor's house, for which he had been ordered to pay fifty dollars—a large sum for him, but his opponent was a rich man and a friend of the alcalde's.

The traders opened their goods at this place; and, as confidence was soon restored, they did a good business, especially by taking corn, wood, hay, cattle, &c., in payment, for these they could again dispose of to the troops. A readiness to sell in this way brought customers from all parts.

As to the wood I purchased, there was a Mexican who used to bring it to me. I knew he came at least thirty miles with it. On my asking him how long he was in coming, he said, one day and a night—rather a tedious journey, to sell only from four to five loads of wood, at from $1.75 to $2 per load; especially as each cart required two men and four yoke of cattle. He could not make much profit.

We were indebted to Señor Ponce, an old Mexican gentleman, and the richest man in the valley of El Paso, for assistance in getting corn and other necessaries for the soldiers. He supplied us, as far as possible, from his own store-houses, and, where these failed, he bought for us.

He stated his income to be about ten thousand dollars a year, which is immense for this part of the country. It arises, principally, from sales of his wine and brandy, both of which are made very largely here. The wine is of a dark-port color, of good quality, and cheap. The brandy has the appearance of gin, but with a pleasing

60 • A Campaign in New Mexico

flavor of its own. It was found, however, to contain a large quantity of copper, from the vessels in which it is made, and wherein it is allowed to stand. This was not discovered until it had affected the health of several of our men. The wine was harmless, being the pure juice of the grape.

As we were still in expectation of being attacked, our men were quartered with regard to defence. Colonel Doniphan's regiments were in two large buildings near the plaza; and our company was in the barracks, to which was attached the calaboose or city jail, so that we were, in reality, in the yard of the latter. This was not very pleasant, but as this building, which was very large, stood on a small eminence in the rear of the church, and could easily be defended by a few resolute men, it was, in spite of the prison, a post of honor. In part of the building was the public school room, well filled with desks and other academical apparatus, but now deserted. I used the room for storing hay and fodder, which created rather a longer holiday than usual. We found schools in most of the towns, as we went from here south.

Colonel Doniphan dispatched a messenger to hasten a company of artillery, which had been previously ordered from Santa Fé; and he determined to await its arrival. Rumors kept reaching us of anticipated resistance at Carrizal—a fortified place some distance on this side of Chihuahua. At last, we found that regular carriers were sent from here to that place; and circumstances led us to suspect Ortis, the priest, of being the agent of the correspondence. A small scouting party was sent, one night, to try to catch him in the act; and there is no doubt he would have been so caught, had it not been for the bad management of the officer in charge, who, instead of waiting to seize the messenger after he might have started, and try to find dispatches upon him, only surrounded the house, went up and politely knocked at the door, in front of which a horse was standing, ready saddled and bridled. Of course, no papers were found, but the priest and two gentlemen were brought up to our colonel's quarters. Ortis was upbraided with treachery;

but he remarked that *he* did not call the delivering his country from a foreign enemy, by any means whatever, treachery. He said he was the enemy of all Americans, and never could be otherwise; and that he should use every endeavor to free his country from them—but that it would be by fair combat, and that he should not attempt to incite an insurrection, knowing that to be worse than useless. Colonel Doniphan told him that he admired his sentiments, but would take care he should have no opportunity to carry them into effect, by keeping a strict watch over him; and that, as he had seen how Mexicans could fight on ground of their own selection—meaning Bracito, where Ortis was—he would take him with him as he went southward, in order that he might observe the Mexicans attacked and made to fight on ground of his, Doniphan's selection. This the colonel did, taking him down to Chihuahua.

The full rascality of the Scotchman whom we had taken the night before the battle, was now made apparent. In the Calaboose we found six Americans who had been confined there for some months. They formed a party whom this fellow had engaged to guide to California; but, instead of this, he took them to El Paso, and there denounced them as Texians. They were thrown into prison, after having been robbed of all they possessed; however, a court of officers acquitted the fellow, and one day I met him going out of town with a parcel upon his back, containing a flask of whisky, a few tortillas and a piece of goat's milk cheese. He was trudging on, he said, to Santa Fé. He had that day been acquitted, and was naturally in some haste to leave our neighborhood, knowing the excitement against him. Never had I felt so strong a desire to commit violence. I advised him to avoid all soldiers, who would shoot him like a dog as he deserved; and I assured him I would do so, if I again met him. His life was not worth a minute's purchase if any of our men were to see him.

The yard in which we were here quartered, had some years before been the scene of a massacre. The governor induced twenty of the chiefs of the Apache Indians to enter it, when they were mur-

62 · A Campaign in New Mexico

dered by soldiers who had been concealed in the buildings. The governor paid the penalty of his treacherous conduct: as he gave the order, "*maten à los carahos!*" (kill the scoundrels!) a chief sprang forward and stabbing him, cried out! "*Entonces moriras tu primero, Carajo!*" (then you shall die first, Carajo!) These Indian warriors died bravely, after killing several Mexicans. This tribe is the most powerful of all the Mexican Indians. It inhabits the range of mountains called the Sierra des Mimbres, which separates the State of Sonora from those of El Paso and Chihuahua—and on each side of this range is its extensive foraging ground;—the country further south being under the control of the Camanches. I do not think the Apache Indians are naturally brave; but having been long unopposed, they have become bold; so much so as to visit large cities amicably, and otherwise in small parties. The fact is, they so heartily despise the Mexicans that they say they would kill them all, were it not that they serve as herdsmen to them—meaning this, that they themselves neither hunt no plant, and being of roving habits, they do not overburden themselves with cattle, preferring to descend from their mountain fastnesses and help themselves out of the first Mexican herd they come across—first killing the herdsmen, if possible. The latter have an instinctive dread of these Indians. The word *Apache* is enough to make a Mexican herdsman tremble, although he goes armed with a sabre, carbine and lance, and is always mounted. One thing which has principally served to make this tribe powerful, is the fact of one state frequently arming it against another.

Some tribes of these Indians live entirely on mule and horse flesh, while others eat the prairie wolf, but there is no doubt they prefer fat cows and steers, frequently running off several thousand head at a time. If a quarrel arises on the foray about the ownership of an animal, they kill the creature, leaving it where it falls, and, of course, the dispute with it. Their track can be traced by this frequent mark of a quarrel.

The government of Chihuahua at one time set a price on every Apache scalp; it was, I believe, one hundred dollars for a man,

CHAPTER FOUR · 63

fifty dollars for a squaw, and twenty-five dollars for a papoose. This plan was afterwards abandoned; and an Irishman, named James Kirker, was hired, at a high salary, to attempt the extermination of the tribe. This was rather an extensive operation, as they numbered about fifteen thousand. However, he, with a band of Americans and Mexicans, soon made the Apaches fear him. The Mexicans look upon him as almost superhuman; but I have heard, from credible authority, that his bravery is rather lukewarm, and that his victories have always been achieved through cunning. He has never risked a fight, unless when his own party has greatly outnumbered the Indians, or when he could catch them asleep—and even then he himself prudently keeps in the back ground. He joined us the morning after the fight of Bracito, having given up hunting the Indians, in consequence of the government having forgotten to pay him. He was very useful to us, serving as guide and interpreter, during all the time we remained in the country. One night, while on our march, three Apache Indians came down and carried off several yoke of oxen and a fine mule, the property of a trader. Lieutenant Jack Hinton took a few men, and followed them for two days, got back the cattle and mule, and killed one of the Indians—bringing in his scalp. At Chihuahua, I found in the Office of the Secretary of State, a mass of letters from prefects of small towns complaining of incursions of these savages—indeed, there was one shelved-side of a room entirely devoted to filed papers on this subject.

Our provisions ran short during our stay at the city of El Paso; and we were obliged to supply ourselves by purchasing from the Mexicans. Wheat I found to be rather scarce. All I could procure, I had ground at a small mill in the city. This was a curiosity. What will our mechanics say to a flouring mill built entirely without iron? All the wheels and other parts were of wood (of course excepting the mere stones, which are made from the ironstone boulders found in all parts of the country). The flour ground by this mill was very coarse, and the bran not separated, but it was much

64 · A Campaign in New Mexico

better than we had been subsisting upon in Santa Fé. There we had been supplied with wheat, first coarsely ground, and then the finest part of the flour sifted out, which, I suppose, the Mexicans used; at any rate, we did not see any of it, and so leaving to us what would be called, in New York, very poor "shorts." I purchased, at different times, some fifteen cattle for slaughter. On averaging their weight, I found it to be only about two hundred and thirty pounds each, when dressed. Although all the Mexican cattle are naturally small, they are beautifully formed, and have the appearance of good weight when on the hoof, but, on cutting them up, they fall off wonderfully. The beef is of excellent quality, except when the animal has been over-driven, and then it becomes speedily poor.

Some of the cattle I bought under rather singular circumstances. One day, the jailor of the prison came and asked me, whether I did not wish to purchase beef-cattle? and on my answering him in the affirmative, he told me that there was a *caballero* in the calaboose, who wished to sell me some. It, of course, struck me as rather a queer place to find a man rich enough to own, and able to sell, cattle. On entering the yard of the prison, I was introduced to a very good-looking, gentlemanly man, who informed me that he was a large cattle owner. After a little bargaining, I bought several beeves of him. On asking the jailor who he was, I was informed that he was one of the richest men in the state, but, being strongly opposed in politics to the ruling authorities, his killing one of his own peons or servants had been taken advantage of to imprison him. "This small peccadillo," added the jailor, "would, under any other circumstances, never have been noticed, and, as he is very rich, he'll soon get out."

One day, while receiving some maize at Don Ponce's country seat, a peon or servant handed me a hot piece of baked pumpkin to taste, which I found delicious, and far superior in flavor to those at home; and I excited much amusement among the peons, who were seated, man, women and children, in the corraal or yard, eating their noon-day meal, by my unaristocratic relish for what is here grown only for the pigs and servants.

CHAPTER FOUR • 65

Colonel Doniphan was a favorite, but truth leads me to mention a circumstance which somewhat shocked my notions of military discipline. A poor Spaniard came to the colonel, and complained that a soldier, standing by, had stolen his pig. The commander turned to the man, and asked him whether this was true? The soldier replied, "Yes;" adding, also, "and pray, Colonel, what are you going to do about it?" This blunt mode of response, mixed with question, rather puzzled Colonel Doniphan, who, after some hesitation, said: "Well! I don't know, unless I come and help you to eat it." I am sadly afraid the complaining party got no redress. I felt it to be a bad example.

So far as our dress was concerned, Falstaff, at this time, would have been ashamed of us. Our hundred men who had last joined were, of course, a little better clad than the rest, but most of the men were in the same clothes in which they had left Missouri six months before—and these had seen pretty severe service in the Navajo country. The best clad were those who had been lucky enough to procure buckskin dresses among the Indians. A parade was now a ludicrous sight. In a whole company, no two pair of pantaloons were of the same hue; and there being few who owned a jacket, the red flannel or checked shirt made up the "uniform." Shoes were a luxury, and hats a very doubtful article. If our habiliments were thus, at this time, what were they further south? If General Taylor could boast of two R's, "Rough and Ready;" we felt that we were fully entitled to three, Rough, Ready and Ragged. We had received no pay as yet; and the sutler charging *ad libitum*.

On the first day of February, 1847, Major Clark and Captain Weightman arrived, bringing with them one hundred and thirty men, four six-pounders, and two twelve-pound howitzers—thus increasing our force to a thousand men. On their arrival, our company was sent to the Presidio del San Elecario, a large fort, standing at the lowest end of the city, where we encamped. This fort has, evidently, been once very strong; and covers more than eight acres of ground. It incloses, within its walls, a pretty church, through which I wandered alone one morning. The Mexicans are jealous of their churches, and do not willingly allow a heretic to enter alone. I lifted up the veils which concealed the different figures in the niches around the walls; and, gazing on their gaudily dressed and painted saintships, I felt that any little girl at home would have been ashamed of such a badly dressed set of dolls.

Leaving the church, I came to the door of the priest's house; and hearing voices, made free to go in. The padre was sitting under the porch, inside of the yard, arguing strenuously with a Spanish merchant. The priest was a good specimen of his species. His exact weight I will not dare to guess, but it was not much less than three hundred pounds. His shaven crown, sandaled feet, dark robe, large wooden rosary and hempen girdle perfected a monk's portrait. He rose, and would not reseat himself until a servant had brought me a stool. We conversed a little in French together, but a woman having carried a substantial breakfast, well set off with plate, into his room, he very soon politely dismissed us both, expressing a wish to see us at some other time. I should have been more impressed with his politeness, if it had embraced an invitation to breakfast.

I walked with the merchant to the Alcalde's office, and found there a respectable-looking couple waiting my companion's return. These people had an only daughter attached to a young neighbor, who had gone, a few days before, to this priest, to obtain permission to marry her. As all the parties were poor, the bridegroom had sold off his three cows to pay the marriage fee; the amount of which not being fixed, the priest has the right to charge whatever he pleases. In this case, he had pocketed the avails of the cows; and then told the bridegroom that he must have much more before he could officiate. The poor lover had stated this to the bride's parents, and they sold off their stock, and paid the priest enough to make about one hundred dollars. His monkship coolly pocketed this also; and then informed the party he had not got near enough yet. In this state of affairs they had applied to the Alcalde for advice, and the merchant, being in the room at the time, had offered to go and remonstrate with the priest, who, however, remained inexorable. After much discussion before the Alcalde, amidst mingled laughter and tears, the bride and bridegroom (who had meanwhile come in), started off home with the old people to get up a fandango, which was to stand in the place of a marriage ceremony—having made up their minds to dispense with the services of the extortionate padre. This little incident may account for the general licentiousness in Mexico. Does not a priest of God thus become a minister of the devil!

CHAPTER FIVE

ON THE ELEVENTH day of February, we started for Chihuahua. The troops left the Rio Grande about thirty miles below fort San Elecario, striking across a dry stretch of ninety miles, entering it on the evening of the fourteenth.

It was on the next day that a mail from Santa Fe overtook us, bringing letters and newspapers. We now first heard that General Wool had changed his route, and that we should not find him at Chihuahua. It was singular enough this mail brought no dispatches for Colonel Doniphan.

In this situation, a council was held; and the question agitated, whether we were to go on to Chihuahua, or turn back to Santa Fe? It was decided to proceed. But we halted while the mail was sorted; and each man, in saddle, received his letters. It was amusing to hear scraps of home news bandied about among my companions. Not having any one to discuss my own letters with me, I left the road, dismounted, sat myself under a large soapweed, and proceeded to read the budget that had fallen to my share. In spite of our rather unpleasant position, in the midst of a dry plain, and already one night and day without water, and with a knowledge that an almost overwhelming force was but a few leagues from us, and no American troops within seven hundred miles, many pleasant jokes connected with our homes were passed this night, and the spirit of our letters kept us cheerfully up to a late hour.

One sad piece of news reached us by this mail—the assassination of Governor Bent at Taos. His death was particularly felt by

69

70 • A CAMPAIGN IN NEW MEXICO

the members of my own mess. Governor Bent had often come amongst us while we were at work at our theatre at Santa Fe, taking a kindly interest in our pleasure, and showing, in many ways, his amiable disposition.

It seems that after the insurgents had seized him, they took him to his own house, and gave him a choice of instant death or the loss of eyes and other atrocious disfigurement. He boldly told them to kill him. To the District Attorney Liel, who had been one of our battalion, they gave no such choice, but used him brutally and killed him piecemeal. We had left some of our company at a grazing ground near Taos; and, therefore, felt great anxiety for them.

From circumstances which have come to my knowledge, I do not consider that the murder of Governor Bent was caused by the insurrection at Taos, but rather that this occurrence was used as a cloak to cover what was, undoubtedly, an act of private malice, instigated by his wife. She was a Spaniard, very beautiful, but had not lived with him for some years, and resided at Taos, where Bent had large properties. There had been several previous attempts to murder him; from one of which he had only escaped by killing his assailant. Bent had been warned never to approach Taos, and this he had not done for some time previous. In order to further her own designs, this woman had taken part in the insurrection—still, so slight a one, that she could not be punished for it.

Soon after our departure from El Paso, two of the traders—all of whom had received positive orders to keep close to us—ventured to lag behind, preferring to await the issue of the approaching contest in safety; and one of them even went so far as to hire a band of Indians to run off his cattle. Colonel Doniphan was rather too old a hand to be thus caught, so he sent Colonel Mitchell with a detachment of men to urge them on. Colonel Mitchell merely told these traders that he would give them one hour to harness-up and proceed, and that if they did not do so in that time, he would string them up to one of the neighboring trees. They rolled their wagons into camp without delay. One of them afterwards ventured to repeat the hesitation to proceed. Colonel Doniphan told the drivers of this trader's wagons, that, from that moment, they were to obey him only, and that he had taken the responsibility to confiscate the goods in them to the United States. However, he afterwards returned them to the owner.

On the seventeenth day of February, we arrived at the remarkable *Lago de los Patos*, Lake of the Ducks, which is about four miles in length, into which several large streams empty, but having no visible outlet. Its water, at most times, is too brackish for use; but now it was fuller than usual from there having been considerable rain in the mountains. This lessened the brackishness; and we found the water very welcome, for our poor animals had been entirely without any for three days and nights, and were almost furious. They instantly filled themselves almost to bursting; and had the water been very salt, it would have injured them.

About a quarter of a mile from this pond, is a singular spring, highly impregnated with sulphur. It rises from the point of a grassy cone, about fifteen feet high, which is as regular in shape as if made by man. The water, although abundant, only runs to the foot of the mound, there sinking into the sand at once. And with the exception of the cone, there is nothing green to be seen in the neighborhood, and this verdure continues the year round.

Soon after we had encamped, a heavy shower of rain came up. It was a blessing to our provision train, which, mostly drawn by oxen, had not yet got through the jornada, and, indeed, never would have got through, had it not been that the rain descended in such torrents as to run in streams across the road, and so enabled the exhausted oxen to drink plentifully, and also stop and rest. It was the opinion of all, that, had it not been for this rain, not a single provision wagon would have ever arrived at the lake.

A few miles to the south, a warm spring rises out of the sand between two small pointed mounds. The water, from its abundance, forms a large stream. The whole bottom of the basin, which is about ten feet across, is in motion from the boiling up of the water. I passed my sabre down through the sandy bottom without the slightest difficulty and struck a rock about three feet below, apparently quite level and extending under the whole basin; yet singularly enough, there is no rock visible around it for some distance.

On the eighteenth, we encamped near the little town of Carrizal, which was, at one time, a principal military post. It has a very large fort, almost equal to that of San Elecario, at El Paso, and which had, until lately, been garrisoned by a large body of Mexican soldiers, who were posted here to protect the surrounding country from the Navajos; but these savages, with their accustomed daring, had laid waste every rancho and house outside of the shadow of the walls, and, in consequence, the inhabitants were fast deserting their homes. In a few years the place will be in ruins. The next day we remained in camp to rest ourselves, and recruit our animals, but experienced the most severe wind-storm I ever witnessed. Tent after tent went down; and if any stood, it was only those which were well lashed with our lassos to sabres and bayonets run into the ground.

On the twentieth, we only marched eight miles, stopping by the side of a deep and swift running stream, made by an immense warm spring which rises about six miles from the road. I did not go to it, but those who did, described it as a most beautiful basin about thirty feet in diameter, pretty deep, and of a very comfortable warmth. Some of my comrades remarked that the water was rather too warm for their liking; and I, myself, observed that even where it crossed our road, it was not quite cold in spite of its six miles run. The channel of this stream, which is narrow, is perfectly straight, and the water runs about four feet from the surface of the ground. What makes it more singular is, that it is supposed to be the water of the river Carmen, which disappears in the sand two or three miles above the spring, and, although cold when it goes into the ground, rises thus hot. I believe that no solution has ever been given for this singularity. Here we cooked for a two days' march, having to cross another jornada of sixty miles in length.

CHAPTER FIVE • 73

However, this was not so bad as usual, as there are holes in a rock about half-way across which generally contain rain water.

We were in constant expectation of being attacked, and, while moving on, had just crossed the dry bed of the Rio Carmen, when an alarm was given that the enemy was coming, and, certainly, a cloud of dust was seen rapidly approaching. So, our advance guard fell back on the main body; and the battery was, at once, unlimbered and everything got ready for action. We had stood thus some minutes, when the cause of alarm turned out to be the dust raised by our own picket guard, which had been stationed six miles on the road above, and, being relieved, had come in to water their horses before starting on the jornada.

Curiosity induced me to wander down the dry bed of the river, which I found to be very wide and sandy. When about a mile from the road, I found, under the roots of an immense oak, which projected from the bank to some distance, a beautiful pool of clear icy-cold water of great depth. It was directly in the sand, which at all other parts, was as level as a floor.

On the evening of the second day, in the jornada, we came to the holes in the rock I have before mentioned, and found them nearly full of water. It was rather bitter to the taste and muddy, and enabled us only to fill our canteens for immediate use and no more. On the afternoon of the next day we discovered water about two miles off the road in a cañon in the mountains, urged by a stiff breeze. I never saw a more beautiful sight than the steady progress at night of that long line of fire—up one surface of an immense mountain by our side, it extended from base to summit; and the timber, in the hollows behind the mountains, having caught, the air was glowing with a rich, red glare, all around.

The next day rumor said that the Mexicans were in great force at the Laguna de Encenillas, which was the real termination of the jornada we were in, and, to reach which, we had to pass one more night without water. Here, it was stated, they intended to await us, expecting that ourselves and our animals would be worn down with thirst.

It would have proved rather a serious business for them, for I believe that men will fight harder when thus suffering from thirst, than from any other excitement. We certainly often felt as if we could have fought Old Nick himself, if he had stood between us and a full canteen. However, when we reached the laguna, our foes had retired. This laguna is a larger pond of water than the Lago de los Patos, but with similar peculiarities of brackishness, shallowness, and having no outlet. We were just making camp, when an accidental fire caught in the grass behind us, and, sweeping towards us with great speed, forced us to harness up our teams again and run. The race lasted two or three miles; and finding that the fire was gaining on us rapidly, the men were dismounted, and placed in a line leading from the lake up to the road, with branches in their hands to beat out the fire at this point, their horses having been first led in a constant string over the line; and in their passage, passing a short distance through the water. The wagons all got over in time. But the artillery had to take refuge, by a quick run, into the lake—frightening thereby a party of Mexican soldiers, who were at a rancho across it, so that they hastened to the mountains and hid themselves, supposing that the artillery were going to charge across the lake, which is in no part very deep. Immediately the fire was checked, we all moved over on to the burnt part, and thus avoided all danger.

On the twenty-sixth, we reached the Rancho of Governor Trias, and found that a large body of the enemy had encamped there the previous night, and had only left at ten o'clock that morning. The Rancheros said that these troops had gone back to Chihuahua; but we afterwards found that they had only withdrawn themselves a little off the road, and had followed us the next day, but had not the spirit to attack our rear, which they had been ordered to do. They had, however, driven off all the beef cattle, except about half a dozen, which we soon slaughtered.

The next day, we only marched a few miles, coming to a few small brackish ponds. Some time was spent in arranging the plan

CHAPTER FIVE · 75

of advance for the morrow—when we should certainly meet the enemy. The wagons, numbering over three hundred, were given in charge of Major Owens, a trader, who formed all his teamsters into two companies, arming them, and explaining to them that, until orders, they were to drive their wagons along in four parallel lines about fifty feet apart, thus forming a rectangle over a quarter of a mile in length, and they were to be all prepared to form a square corral or fort with the wagons for the soldiers, should it prove necessary.

This evening, Captain Skillman and another trader had chased a Mexican spy so hard as to force him to dismount, and seek safety on foot. They brought in the horse, beautifully equipped with silver mounted saddle and bridle, and fine holster pistols. Our picket-guard also, on going out after dark to take up their position, had driven in the advance guard of our foe, although twice their number.

The next morning, Sunday, the twenty-eighth of February, we moved out of camp, the wagons first taking up the positions fixed upon the evening previous; and the artillery occupying the centre space between the two battalions of Doniphan's regiment, who filled the two outside spaces. Our company marched ahead of the now solid square.

Although I was very unwell, and almost unable to ride, I had gone forward with three others to reconnoitre; and getting upon some rising ground, with the aid of a telescope, I obtained a fine view of the whole of the Mexican force; and I do not hesitate to say that, as I turned from viewing that dense mass of soldiery to look at our little band as it came slowly but steadily on, my heart felt a little faint. I could see the numerous entrenchments and batteries of the Mexicans; and I observed to myself, that there was but one way by which we could possibly fight them on at all even ground—and this was, by crossing a deep gully, when we should get upon a grassy plain, extending with a slight ascent up to their position. On all other sides the high bluff bank forbade all attempt.

I rejoined our company; and found that Colonel Doniphan had resolved to attack: following exactly the route I have above mentioned. And now, spades and pickaxes are put in requisition, and numerous willing hands soon fill up the gully.

As our troops cross it, the trumpets sound the *Trot*. All move out from the cover of the wagons, and take up a position about nine hundred yards from the most advanced of the enemy, and, from the sloping ground, rather below them. Nothing can exceed the enthusiasm of the men—one would suppose they are rather thinking of getting up a fandango, than of going into such an unequal fight. That overwhelming force in their front had no other effect than to raise their spirits still higher.

But slowly and majestically above our heads, sails America's bird, a large bald eagle.—"An omen, an omen," runs through our ranks, and all eyes glance at him for a moment.

Our little battery occupies the centre of our position—on the right and left of it are two companies of cavalry, one of them Col. Mitchell's escort, and behind them, dismounted and acting as infantry, impatiently stand the rest of Doniphan's regiment.

As we form, the enemy's artillery opens upon us, and, at that instant, Weightman's clear voice is heard—"Form battery, action front, load and fire at will;" and our pieces ring out the death-knell of the enemy; now comes the friendly struggle between our gunners, who shall pour in the deadliest and quickest fire, and beautifully are those pieces served, mowing lane after lane through the solid columns of the Mexicans. In the centre of the battery, their horses bounding at every discharge, stand Clark and his officers. As the balls fly through the opposing ranks, and the shells tear their columns, shout after shout is heard from our men.

Further to our right sits Colonel Doniphan on his beautiful chestnut charger, with his leg crossed over the saddle, steadily whittling a piece of wood, but with his eye glancing proudly over the ranks of his little band. As the cannonading becomes hotter, he quietly says: "Well, they're giving us ———— now, boys!" and

CHAPTER FIVE • 77

passes coolly to the left of our position, untouched by the copper hail that pours around him.

And here *we* are (at a distance too great for anything but cannon), sitting on our horses dodging Mexican balls as they come humming through our ranks, first striking the ground about midway, and so becoming visible. It was surprising the skill which we soon obtained in this employment. After a few shots, we could tell to a foot where the copper messenger would alight; although, a few minutes before, joke after joke was passing among us, the silence was now almost unbroken, for nothing acts so well, by way of a safety valve to a man's courage, as having to sit on horseback half an hour and dodge cannon balls. As yet we know of no injuries amongst us, but suddenly, a German close by, blurts out "I'se kilt," and, tumbling off his horse, rolls up his trowsers, showing a severe contusion on his leg, caused by a stone thrown up by the ricochet of a cannon-ball; round the limb goes a handkerchief, and up mounts the man again. At that moment a groan bursts from the line to my left, and a man is borne dying from the ranks, while off goes the head of Lieutenant Dorn's horse. Hot work on all sides!

So confident are the Mexicans, that some of the richest citizens of Chihuahua have come out as spectators; but now, judging wisely, off they fly at full speed to the city, giving notice of the probable result, but are so little believed that, like true prophets before them, they are actually stoned in the streets.

A shell explodes directly in the ranks of the enemy—they draw back behind their entrenchments—and we immediately advance until within four hundred yards—again the deadly shower opens from our ranks, fiercely returned. The order to charge rings through our line—Colonel Mitchell, on his favorite white charger Roderick, waves his sabre as he leads us on; rumbling and crashing behind us comes Weightman with his howitzers, leaving the rest of the battery in position to cover our advance. Dashing past us goes Major Owens, waving his hand in an exulting manner, and shouting out, "Give it to them, boys! they can't withstand us"—and away he

78 · A Campaign in New Mexico

goes: falling, in two minutes a corpse, struck in the forehead by a grape-shot while storming the redoubts, and being so close to the gun that the fire actually burns his clothes. Rapidly is our charge made; but just fairly under way, it is about to be ruined! A countermanding order, as if from Doniphan, is given by a drunken officer whose rank (alone) requires respect. In surprise we suddenly halt within a few yards of the redoubts, and are fully exposed to the whole of the enemy's fire. "For God's sake, advance!" roars out our sutler Pomeroy, who was fighting in the ranks—our hesitation vanishes, and away we instantly dash forward, gallantly led by Mitchell and Gilpin, while Weightman fires his howitzers loaded with canister, with great effect, and again advancing, wheels them to the right and left, throwing in another charge of grape and canister and raking the whole line of the enemy's position. To our left is a battalion of brave cavalry, from Durango, who have arrived on the field only half an hour before—'tis their last fight—they are terribly cut to pieces, and are forced to retreat. A piece of their artillery, being dismounted, they attempt to "snake," by fastening their lassos to it, and drag it along the ground, but they are overtaken and made prisoners, and the gun is ours. Our men, pouring over the embankments, actually push the Mexicans out. Now comes the rout; the Mexicans give way; and *sauve-qui-peut* is their only object. We are in possession of their main position. The rest of our battery comes galloping up to occupy it. A body of their lancers reforms and prepares to renew the attack—but—they are soon sent after their flying companions. We are about congratulating ourselves on a victory: when—bang goes a cannon, and a ball bounds amongst us, knocking the saddle-blanket off the mule of one of our company, from which he has this instant dismounted. A cloud of white smoke curls gracefully upwards from a hitherto masked battery to the right upon yon high mountain, as shot after shot falls amongst us. Two of our six pounders are at once placed in one of the deserted entrenchments and commence a well directed fire, which soon dismounts one of the enemy's pieces. Up

CHAPTER FIVE • 79

charges Mitchell at the head of his company, and takes the position; yet down, with headlong speed, dashes an officer waving a Mexican flag—one of our gunners points his cannon at him—a moment and he would have been no more, but his horse is recognized, 'tis Colonel Mitchell's Roderick, while the Colonel himself is the standard bearer.

Numerous skirmishes occur as pursuit takes the place of resistance. Weightman dashes on with the cavalry towards the city. Looking over his shoulder, he sees his howitzers halted on the hill side instead of following him, and galloping back, he shouts "On with that battery; if I knew who had halted you, I'd cut him down." The officer who had done so said not a word.

But the battle is won. And gradually we assemble on the battlefield. The enemy are fast disappearing in the distance, baffling pursuit.

And what has, all this time, been the conduct of the priest Ortis and the three other Spaniards we brought down to see the fight? At the commencement of the struggle, they stand up in their light carriage, to which two mules are attached, and which still remains in the centre of our wagon columns. Seeing the dense mass of their countrymen, they cannot contain their joy—the first few shots are exchanged.—Ortis and his three companions are still standing in the vehicle with outstretched necks and eager eyes.—But see— the Mexican columns waver, and rank after rank bites the dust,— at last, they fly—the countenances of the priest and his companions fall, their bright visions vanish, and, jumping out, they run behind that very large wagon-wheel. Good men, they are praying and telling their beads with unusual rapidity, with trembling voices and shaking hands. A sad task was the priest's that night, and many a poor Mexican soldier died murmuring his confession into his ear.

Recognitions and congratulations take place. "Why, I heard you were killed!" is said by one to another, until after everybody had shaken hands with almost everybody, and then the question arose, who was killed? For, with the exception of Major Owens, we had not lost a man! but the dead and the dying of the enemy were all around us. It is true, that we had several severely wounded, and many slightly; and as the shot fired at us was of copper, we were afraid we should lose many of our wounded; but three only, as I understand, have since died.

On examining the ground we had won, it seemed almost impossible to believe that, in only three hours, we had beaten such a large force, holding so excellent a position, the hill which they had chosen giving them the advantage of ground on all sides, and commanding all three roads into Chihuahua. There were five large circular redoubts, connected by long entrenchments for infantry between; the whole number of redoubts and entrenchments was twenty-eight, and these were defended by ten pieces of four, six, and nine pound-artillery, with six musquetoons or escopetas, carrying one pound lead balls. Several loads of ammunition were left behind; and among the spoil were nine wagon loads or about thirteen thousand pounds of hardbread, four loads of dried meat, weighing over sixteen thousand pounds, and any quantity of sweetened flour for making atole, besides over seven hundred thousand cigaritos, several thousand head of cattle, and ten *acres* of sheep.

I have said that the dead and dying Mexicans were around us; but having found, in their medical wagon, a quantity of excellent litters, we had all the wounded brought in. Their surgeon, who was a prisoner, was requested to attend to them, but he obstinately refused; and numbers bled to death that night from inattention. Our men showed their natural goodness of heart by the kind attention they paid to them; and the next morning, our own surgeon dressed their wounds. I was much struck with one of the prisoners, who was secretary and aide-camp to the Governor, Angel Trias; he was a Spaniard, and a very handsome man, both in face and figure. He had received a rifle ball in the small of the back, which had passed through just inside the spine, thus making an exceedingly painful, although not dangerous wound. He had evidently had enough of fighting Americans: and afterwards, while

CHAPTER FIVE • 81

recovering at Chihuahua, was much pleased when any of us would visit him. The enemy lost, in killed and wounded, about eleven hundred men, besides a considerable amount of property. Several of our soldiers found large sums of money at the camp, in the trunks of the officers, which they broke open. There must have been over fifty thousand dollars, altogether; and as every man kept his own counsel, it was not recovered.

I found a white flag on the battle field; and one of our men picked up the black flag that had been brought out to us at Bracito. It was brought home by Major Clark, who still retains it. Several national and regimental colors were also taken.

In one of the wagons, left behind by the Mexicans, were several bundles of rope, cut into short convenient pieces. These had been provided to tie us when we should have been conquered. There were also great quantities of small bags, which a Mexican officer told us were to have been filled with cotton, and hung around the necks of their soldiers, as a sort of protective armor;—they must have heard of General Jackson and the cotton bags at New Orleans.

In a hollow near the Mexican camp, we found a large wagon, with the mules ready harnessed; but one of the animals was killed by a cannon ball. Under the wagon a fire was kindled, and some of our men, lifting the cover, saw several wounded Mexicans lying in it, whom they helped out, after kicking away the fire, which had almost burned through the bottom. Among those in the wagon, to our astonishment, we found an old acquaintance; being no other than the sergeant whom I mentioned as being cured of three bullet holes through his intestines at Bracito. This time he had not come off so well, as both of his legs were shot off. He died in the hospital at Chihuahua. Under these poor fellows, we found about three pounds of fine Kentucky rifle powder, which the enemy, being unable to carry off, on account of the wounded mules, had thus attempted to destroy,— fifteen minutes more, and the poor wounded Mexicans would have been blown to atoms.

82 • A CAMPAIGN IN NEW MEXICO

I should have mentioned, that about a month before, a notice had been forwarded by Colonel Doniphan to the Governor of Chihuahua, that if he did not come out and fight us in open field, he would burn the city. They had, accordingly, come out here with French engineers, and erected their defences: and no place could have been better adapted for it. If two thousand Americans were to occupy this position, no five thousand men could drive them from it; but we had not more than nine hundred in the action, yet drove more than four thousand out. I saw their Adjutant General's book, which showed their force to be four thousand two hundred men, commanded by "Generals Heredia; Garcia Conde; Angel Trias, Governor of Chihuahua; and Cuilty."

A detachment was at once sent on to the city, to secure it, and to send the alcalde to bury the dead, which he did, by having them thrown into the trenches, and tumbling the embankments upon them. Little did those now under them think, when throwing up the redoubts, that they were digging their own graves.

I have understood that, as we started on the charge, Colonel Doniphan covered his face with his hands, and almost groaned out, "My God! they're gone! the boys will all be killed!" Then instantly raising his head, he struck his spurs into his horse's sides, and came dashing after us.

We encamped upon the battle field this night. The next day, we marched but a few miles; and the day after brushed ourselves up for a triumphal march into Chihuahua. My company carried in the captured banners and lances, and I had the honor of bearing one of the Mexican national flags, now, however, closely gathered round its staff, and not flaunting the air as it had done the day it was borne out of the city. In our line, were all the captured artillery and other trophies.

The road, by which we approached the city, was thickly strewed with fragments of arms and other military things, showing the haste with which the Mexicans had fled.[*]

---

[*]See the official account of the battle in the Appendix, No. 2.

CHAPTER SIX

THE SIDE from which we entered the city presented the worst view of it; and it was not until we had traversed a long distance of suburbs with immense piles of scoria alternating with mean houses that we came to any good looking dwellings. But a course which took us past the unfinished Jesuit's College, the plaza and fine cathedral, and through nicely paved streets to the Alameda or public walk, soon showed us that we had got into a city far superior to any place we had before entered. Most of the houses had white stone fronts; while the paved streets and good side walks made it somewhat home like, for we had seen no pavement before since leaving Missouri.

We were quartered at the Plaza de Toros or Bull Ring. This is a fine amphitheatre, and being government property, it is built in the best manner, with several rows of white stone seats all round, and a covered gallery above and at the back of them. The ring itself is more than one hundred yards in diameter, and the whole building, which is square externally, is very high and handsomely decorated. In front of this, and extending the whole length of the city, is the public Alameda handsomely planted with rows of cotton wood trees and streams of water running through it; and here and there white stone seats. In the middle of the city is the plaza or square, and in the centre of this is a public fountain, to which the water is brought from falls about six miles below. The plaza is surrounded by numerous handsome resting placcs, or rather large stone sofas. Fronting it towards the north is a large building con-

83

taining the public granary and Congress Hall—the former of which is very extensive and well fitted up, and in it we found a large quantity of maize and beans. The Congress Hall consists of a beautiful room, with a railed enclosure at one end, in which sat their legislature, and at the top of the table, under a canopy, used to preside the Governor. Behind his seat is a large painting representing Iturbide, Hidalgo and Morelos, the latter in the act of being crowned by liberty, while under their feet lies a Spanish soldier, with sundry broken fetters and whips. Around the upper part of the room, is a gallery with a gilt railing. I sat down in the chair which Governor Trias occupied, when the legislative body decided what should be our fate when taken: which was, after being stripped of money and arms, to be sent on foot to the city of Mexico. Attached to the hall are numerous rooms, with such designations on the doors as showed them to have been occupied by judges and officers of state. In front of the building runs a wide colonnade, between the pillars of which we placed our battery. Attached to the water spouts in front, I remarked several Apache scalps, relics of some unusually successful skirmish. On the western side of the plaza stands the treasury building, very massive, with numerous handsome rooms, which we used as quarters for some of our companies.

On the south side, is a building of which the inhabitants are justly proud, the cathedral. Its exterior is covered with fine carving and statues. The front has three tiers of pillars, one above another, with figures of Christ and the twelve Apostles in different niches the size of life. Its two steeples, which are square and composed of pillars fancifully carved, were, a short time before, hung with bells; but the inhabitants had cleared one of the steeples, in order to use the metal in making cannon. The edifice stands upon a raised terrace well walled around. The next day after we had entered, I had an opportunity of seeing the inside of the building; and although most of the valuable articles had been removed, yet the interior fully realized my expectations. It is lighted only from the dome, which is very large and gayly painted. Around the walls are six large shrines reaching to the ceiling, and resembling highly decorated chapel fronts, richly gilded, and having wax images and artificial flowers enclosed within glass or gratings. The altar is not handsome; nor did I at any time see upon it much plate and gold or silver emblems. This cathedral cost two millions of dollars, and was some thirty years in building. The occasion on which I first visited it was, however, a very melancholy one. In the centre of the church lay the body of Major Owens. He having been a Catholic, the priests had willingly offered to inter him. It was sad to know that, under that velvet pall, lay the man who had so exultingly dashed before us in the charge a few days before!

Perhaps nothing could have been better calculated to allay the terror and dislike of the citizens, than to see their priests thus performing funeral service over one of our officers. At the head of the coffin stood a high pyramidal stand, covered with velvet, and upon it wax candles in silver sconces set all over it; the priests were in full canonicals of velvet and gold, chanting the mass; while round them knelt numerous Mexicans, and outside them were our men standing closely together. At the end of the usual church service, the priests all marched in procession round the church, preceded by a man wearing a green mantle, with a red heart embroidered upon the left breast, who, being the sexton, would occasionally raise a smile on our heretic faces, by stopping the procession to drive out some intruding dog.

I do not think I have previously spoken of the immense number of dogs in Mexico,—it seems to me beyond calculation; and being almost all a cross of the prairie wolf, have an exceedingly mean appearance. I did not see a gentlemanly dog in all Mexico. The pet dogs are called "Comanche;" but why I know not. They are without any hair, and of a dark slate color; and to me, the nastiest animals I know of to look at or to feel. And as to the dogs in general, I should advise a traveller never to stir out without a revolving pistol. The dogs have as strong a dislike to it as their mas-

86 · A Campaign in New Mexico

ters, and the possession alone will be a sufficient safeguard from either cur or owner.

A short distance down one of the streets leading from the plaza, stands the unfinished college chapel of San Francisco, begun by the Jesuits some years before their expulsion, and not finished on account of that event (which occurred in 1767). The chapel remains as they left it looking like some enormous skeleton rising from a heap of ruins. This appearance arises from several slender arches of large span, which were to have supported the roof, but now stand alone, although the stone composing them is not more than two feet square. The front and one of the side entrances are finished, and give good evidence that, had the Jesuits been allowed to complete the building, it would have been very grand and pure in design. Numerous statues adorn the outside; but within, there have lately been erected two large furnaces, in which were melted the bells and other metal for the cannon we had taken from them, and which were cast in a large pit in the floor of the building. The smoke from these furnaces has blackened all the inside of such part as was finished, and given it a very singular appearance. Adjoining the chapel is the Jesuits' Hospital, a large and very complete building, and to which we removed our sick and wounded. In this building had once been imprisoned the patriot Hidalgo, who was shot in the square in the rear. And here, too, Kendall and his party had been confined. On the spot where Hidalgo fell, is erected a high monument, which would be handsome were it not that the obelisk part is painted in flames; rather a sinister compliment to the spirit of the Catholic patriot. On the four sides are long inscriptions, two to Hidalgo, one to Iturbide, and one to the glorious sixteenth day of September, 1810, the day of Mexican Independence.

In my rambles about the streets, I observed, in most of them, splashes of blood, evidently caused by some wounded soldier hastily dismounting. One can imagine this bloody messenger from the field, hurriedly telling of defeat.

CHAPTER SIX • 87

Let me here correct a statement made in the public papers. It is said that our artillery, at the battle of Sacramento, was drawn by oxen. No so, our American horses, and fine horses they were, were employed, while mules drew our caissons.

I have the following second-hand, and yet there is no reason to doubt it. During our march from El Paso to Chihuahua, the black servants of the different officers of the regiment formed themselves into a company. There were twelve of them, of which number eleven were officers, and one high private. Jo ____, servant to Lieut. D ____, was elected Captain. He was the blackest of the crowd, and sported a large black feather with a small black hat— also, a large sabre, with an intensely bright brass hilt—which same sabre was eternally getting involved with the intricate windings of his bow legs. With Jo for captain they were a formidable body, and to hear them talk, they would work wonders! During the battle of Sacramento, however, the company was not to be seen; but after the action was over, they were espied breaking out from the wagons, and joining in the pursuit. That evening, one of our officers attacked Jo about his company.

"Well, Jo, I hear your men were hid behind the wagons during the fight?"

"Lieutenant, I'se berry sorry to say it am de truf! I done eberyting—I call'd on de paterism ob de men—I injoked dem by all dey hold most deah in dis world and de nex, but it was no go— dey would get on de wrong sides ob de wagons."

"But what did *you* do there?"

"I stood dar gittin' cooler, and de firing kept gittin' hotter, and at last de cannon balls cum so ormighty fass, I thought de best ting dis nigga could do, war to get behind de wagons heself!"

I found, in the Secretary of State's office, where we were quartered, among other papers, a government extra, showing most accurately our force and strength, but interlarded with peculiarly Mexican untruths; a translation is in the Appendix No. 3.

88 · A Campaign in New Mexico

Ortis and his companions were released immediately we arrived at Chihuahua; and they stated, when they got back to El Paso, that we had not fought like men, but like wolves and tigers.

While we stayed in Chihuahua, a bull fight was got up for our amusement. But the bulls named Ampudia, Ponce de Leon, and so on, had been too much starved to show fight, and it was difficult to get them to attack the matadores. Many cock-fights took place, at which much money changed hands.

Blessings on the Chihuahuans, for their light bread and sweet cakes. It was a great treat to the volunteer, after walking to the market early in the morning, and purchasing this bread and a lump of butter, to enjoy both with a cup of coffee. They have a singular mode of putting up their butter; it is in lumps the size and shape of a hen's egg wrapped round with the shuck of the Indian corn, and each two lumps fastened together. As the inhabitants never use salt, from its high price, the butter does not keep long. I here purchased some salt for our troops, and had to pay no less than fifteen dollars for each fanega, equal to seven dollars a bushel; and this was of the coarsest kind and was more than half lime. And yet I only paid the customary price. It is brought all the way from El Poso, although there is, in fact, plenty around Chihuahua, but the Apaches will not let the inhabitants collect it—indeed, these savages have stopped the working of all the mines, by driving the miners away.

Crossing a valley about three miles from the city, are numerous very tall arches supporting the aqueduct, which conducts the water to the fountain in the plaza. By some freak of the architect, two of the arches are imperfect, being made to incline in opposite directions, and giving it a very singular appearance.

Just below the dam which throws the water into this aqueduct is a beautiful natural fall in the stream. It is not high, but at the point of a cleft, the water tumbles down between the rocks with great noise.

I may here remark, upon the spinning of the coarse wool of the Mexican sheep by the women of the lowest orders. They may be seen constantly seated on the floor twirling, with great dexterity, a

CHAPTER SIX • 89

spindle, set in a shallow saucer upon the ground, and twisting the yarn between the left finger and thumb; and it is surprising with what dexterity they will thus spin a coarse yarn, or, rather, what is called by our spinners, a sliver, which is used in the manufacture of their blankets.

The ridiculous fool-hardiness of our men was illustrated one day, by the following incident. I was superintending the unloading of an ammunition wagon by some of our own men, and was receiving the powder, &c., in a small room, in which lay more than two hundred cannon cartridges, besides other ammunition, when one of the men very coolly walked in with a key of powder on his shoulder and a lighted pipe in his mouth! and asked me to lift it down for him; on remonstrating with him, he expressed the greatest surprise at my remarks; this is only one case out of a dozen. They seemed to be entirely devoid of fear, but I am not ashamed to say that *I* felt very uncomfortable when the man walked into the room.

The mint here is very extensive, and under contract by an Englishman, named Potts, who made himself conspicuous by threatening us with the displeasure of his government. Colonel Mitchell was desirous of examining the residence of Governor Trias, who had fled; and understanding that Mr. Potts had the key, he sent for and told him that it was necessary he should take up his residence in the mansion for a few days, in order to examine any papers there at his leisure. But Potts became angry, and told the Colonel that the key had been entrusted to him, and he should not give it up. On being assured that the door would be broken open, he said that being a British subject he considered the house under the protection of the British flag, and that any violence to it would be resented by his government. Colonel Mitchell, who was standing in front of the house, turned to me and told me to collect what men I could find in the streets, and send up for a howitzer with which to blow open the door. I did so immediately; and in a few minutes two howitzers arrived, and were pointed at the huge portal. At this moment, out came running Mrs. Potts from her own house, exclaiming, "Don't fire! don't fire! perhaps my brother is behind that door!" Colonel Mitchell told her that nothing should prevent him blowing the doors down, if Mr. Potts did not produce the key, and he now meanly said he had lost it. Some of our men clambered over a side wall and broke open the doors from the inside. On that day, "Pedrigo Potts was *not* a happy man!"

Soon after we entered Chihuahua, our company were set to work making cartridges for our captured cannon; and it certainly would have frightened any nervous man to have seen the quantity of gunpowder strewed through our building day after day. I believe there was more than five hundred pounds of loose powder standing in boxes or scattered about, and subject, at any moment, to a chance spark of fire—several of our men occasionally passing over it with lighted cigars.

While we were in this city, a Council of War was called. We had expected to have here met and joined General Wool; however, we had done our work without him; but what course were we now to take? for there was danger at all points! A few of the officers proposed staying in Chihuahua, others were for trying to join General Taylor, and some suggested a retrograde march to Santa Fé; most, however, were in favor of pressing home by way of Monterey. No ultimate decision was at that time had; but a short time afterwards, another council was held, and, at this time, most of the officers were for remaining in quarters. Doniphan heard them for some time, but with impatience, and at last, bringing his heavy fist down on the table, he gave the board to understand that they might possibly have found *fair* reasons for staying, "but gentlemen," added the Colonel, *"I'm for going home to Sarah and the children."* The reader may be assured that we caught up these words, and often afterwards spoke of "going home to Sarah and the children."

On the fifth of April, the artillery, with one battalion of Colonel Doniphan's regiment, started for Parral, a large town where the state government had established itself, after its expulsion from the city of Chihuahua; but, on the third day out, some Americans

CHAPTER SIX • 91

came up, bringing news that the frightened Governor had broken up his government and fled to the city of Mexico—so there was a return to old quarters.

The next day, an express of twelve men was sent down to General Taylor for orders, which were to decide whether we would at once go home by the way of Texas, or join him. The express returned on the twenty-fourth of April, bringing orders for us to join General Taylor at once, *via* Parras and Saltillo.

On Sunday, the twenty-fifth, we bid farewell to the city of Chihuahua, where we had been quartered more than a month. The thick-headed Mexicans, who had all been living on us, made night hideous by their rejoicing cries and bell ringing. Their principal shout was, "The *gringoes* are gone, hurrah!" This word "gringo," is a corruption of "greenhorn," and is supposed by the Mexicans to be the most opprobrious American term they can use, equal to the word *chivo* with them, which means a he-goat. You may call a Mexican by any term of reproach but this—use *chivo*, even to a common beggar, and you will put him into a most tremendous passion.

It is utterly impossible for any one who has not seen it, to imagine the difference which exists between the rich and the poor in this wretched country. The rich, who rule everything—even the minds of the poor—are generally most debased in all moral sense, and become, from their brutality, cruel masters. And having, too, the power to punish to any extent save death, they are served with the most abject deference by their peons or servants. These, mostly bound to them by some debt which the master takes care the poor fellow shall not be enabled to pay, appear to have neither mind nor hope above their present condition, and will continue to work on, from day to day, and from year to year, without receiving more than enough to keep body and soul together. There is nothing they will not do for a little money, even to the sale of wives and daughters. The religious feeling which pervades all classes, young and old, is remarkable. Never do you see any of them pass a church without uncovering their heads and turning their faces thitherward, while, at the sound of the bell for vespers, every hat is removed and all stand uncovered where they are, until the sound is over, when each one resumes whatever he may have been doing when interrupted.

The whole country to the south of Chihuahua swarmed with small black and yellow lizards which started from under our horses' feet in all directions; they moved with remarkable rapidity, and it was difficult to catch them. Their number was so great at times, as to give a seeming living motion to the ground.

Our first encampment was at a most beautiful rancho. All the buildings were of white stone. It was part of the estate of a French-man, lately deceased, who had been, for many years, a resident of Chihuahua. The next day we passed a deserted rancho. It had been attacked by the Apache Indians a very short time before, and the dead undestroyed bodies lying around, showed the cruelty of the assailants. Let me here observe, that I have mentioned before how the wolves were said to have scratched up the dead bodies, after the battle and their burial at Bracito. I did not mean to have it also inferred, that the wolves had devoured the dead Mexicans, for it is a curious fact that the wolf will not eat the Mexican—the red pepper, which makes a mummy of the latter, is also said to make the flesh too high-seasoned for the former. Only think of an epicurean wolf!

We were obliged, from the entire want of grass south of Chihua-hua, to purchase the standing wheat as fodder for our horses; and where we encamped away from any village, our poor animals had to live on the maize alone, which sadly heated them with fever.

A few days afterwards, we encamped at Santa Cruz, a fine town, and near which is a large hacienda or country seat, where I found a good cotton mill, fitted up with American machinery. I never saw a finer water-wheel than that attached to this mill. Here I also observed the first cotton growing.

On the thirtieth, we reached San Rosalia, where we saw an-other specimen of Mexican folly, in an immense unfinished fort,

CHAPTER SIX • 93

which was commenced to repel General Wool, who was expected to come by this route to Chihuahua. What could ever make them believe that Wool would take the trouble to attack a fort posted where this was, when he could marshall round it out of gun shot, I cannot imagine! At this place, large quantities of a coarse liquor, called mescal, are manufactured from the Maguey plant or Agave Americana, which is largely cultivated at all the southern villages, although it grows in a wild state in all parts below Chihuahua. In order to obtain the liquor from this aloe, the leaves are cut off level with the ground, and then the root is dug up. The latter is about the size and shape of a quart bowl and is, of a dry woody texture; but, on being piled in large heaps, and roasted, it becomes very juicy and tender, and of a sweet taste. The roots are then pressed, and the liquor allowed to ferment; after fermentation, it resembles beer in appearance, and somewhat in taste, but a little smoky, and is called pulque. It is drunk very extensively by the lower classes. From the pulque there is distilled a clear colorless liquor, of a most acrid and burning taste, which is the mescal. It is only fit for a Mexican to drink—he can do it without winking; but I shall never forget a glass of it which I swallowed at San Rosalia, and which was considered of an extra good quality. It appeared to draw my tongue half way down my throat, and took my breath away for an instant. It was the first and last glass of mescal I ever drank.

Our next camp was at Guajaquilla, where we had to prepare for another of those dry jornardas—sixty miles across. We encamped upon it but once, travelling all the second night, and late on the second day reached San Berrardo, where we got only brackish water, strongly impregnated with sulphur. On a hill rises a large fine spring, cool and pretty good, but the water, disappearing before it gets down the hill, re-appears in the valley in numerous deep holes, very much the worse in quality for its subterranean journey.

The next night we encamped below the walls of Fort Pelayo, which crowns the top of a very high conical hill, almost impregnable from its position. And here were posted some Mexican sol-

94 · A Campaign in New Mexico

diers. However, they were only to keep the Indians off. Colonel Mitchell, who had preceded us by one day's march, with a small escort, had surrounded the place the day before and disarmed the soldiers, surprising their commander in bed, but had returned the men their guns, on their word not to use them against Americans. This sort of treatment astonished them exceedingly, but it no doubt had a very good effect on the surrounding inhabitants.

Our men this night gave loose to their foraging propensities, by slaughtering almost all the pigs, fowls and young calves in the village below the fort. I never saw our soldiers act so before—they had invariably treated the people with great forbearance—always paying for what they took. But, to-night, the spirit of destruction seemed to seize on all, while no effort was made to repress the outbreak. From remarks made, all the fowls were supposed to have been cleared off, but a companion told me, he positively, in the morning, heard the crowing of one solitary cock!

At Fort Pelayo is a very large warm spring of pure water, which runs along the ground for about a quarter of a mile, and then tumbles, suddenly, into a hole. Where it goes to, I do not know; but it was the subject of remark that so much warm water and sulphur as we had seen and smelt for the last two days seemed to betoken a contiguity to a certain place of punishment, while, as long as this spring continued to run, there would be no want of water down below.

The next night we encamped at Rancho Cadena, the owner of which, having heard of our foray on the pigs and chickens of the previous evening, rode out to meet us, and offered us whatever we might require of wood and corn, if we would respect his property. This was readily agreed to. At his house we found a two-pounder cannon, very handsomely mounted in heavy field-piece style, and evidently new. The owner assured us, however, that it was only got to resist Apache Indians and not American citizens; and he was allowed to keep his cannon. Encamped here, we found an old Mexican with a hundred pack-mules laden with common corn

CHAPTER SIX • 95

sugar, which he was taking to the upper countries to sell, having accumulated the money which he had earned while carrying goods from Matamoros to General Taylor's camp. He spoke in the highest terms of old Rough and Ready, but I believe that good prices *here* gave the veteran a good character.

After this, we came to the small village of Mapimi, then almost deserted. As this was in the state of Durango, the government had adopted a real Mexican mode of keeping up appearances. In order to get to Parras, where we were to await further orders, it was necessary to cross this upper eastern corner of Durango; but which, as we had no idea of conquering the whole state, was though rather impudent, and, therefore, four thousand valiant dragoons were sent to Mapimi to follow us through the state, and then to come back and boast how they had chased the Yankees through the glorious and invincible state of Durango; of course, ending their report in the usual Mexican style, "Dios-y-Libertad!" All this they carried out to the letter. They encamped in the mountains about six miles from the town, until we had left it.

The poor inhabitants, who had fled from their homes by order of the government, had ascended the sides of the mountains; and their fires were to be seen like stars on the dark hill sides. However, we had just received the news of the taking of Vera Cruz, and, about nine o'clock, we fired a salute in honor of General Scott's victory. It was laughable to see the lights on the mountains go out, one after another, their watchers evidently thinking we were about sending them iron messengers. I could imagine the terror of the poor people while waiting, breathlessly, for the expected ball to strike some of them, and the relief they must have felt when the salute was over. By the time the last gun was fired, there was not a spark to be seen in the mountains. Silence and darkness were with the unhappy dwellers there.

The next night we had just encamped, after a ride of forty miles, when a Spaniard dashed into camp, and, in a breath, stated that the four thousand Mexican troops were going to cut off the traders, who had lagged behind us this day. As to the traders and their goods, I know not but that they would have been left to their fate, had it not been known that two of them, Magoffin and another, had their wives with them, and that these were American ladies. Half an hour had not elapsed before two hundred and fifty men were galloping back to their relief; that number being modestly considered as sufficient to beat off the four thousand. But for some reason, the traders were not attacked, and got safely into camp about twelve o'clock at night.

Our next encampment was at San Lorenzo, on the banks of the Nazas river. Here I purchased as pretty a white pony as ever I saw for fifteen dollars. Two days afterwards, on reaching a large rancho called El Poso, we found, lying just outside of the walls, some dozen naked bodies of Indians, badly cut up by rifle balls. The mystery was soon explained:—a band of about sixty Lipans, (a branch of the Camanches,) had been observed coming up the valley from San Luis Potosi, with many stolen horses and captive Mexicans. A guard, that had preceded us, with Colonel Mitchell, was then in Parras, twenty-five miles off; and the owner of El Poso, knowing that the savages would attack his rancho, went to the men composing Mitchell's guard, and offered each one the use of a good pony to go up and repel them. About a dozen agreed to do so, and having ridden nearly all night, arrived just before daylight at the estate. Soon afterwards, a small party from our troops, principally officers, who had left the main body early that morning, to push on to Parras by the evening, came up, thus increasing the force to twenty, who, as soon as it was daylight, perceived the Indians advancing up the valley. As they came in front of the buildings, the Americans sallied out, and took up a position in front of them; and, after receiving a heavy flight of arrows, fired a volley at the Indians, which, apparently, did no harm, as they kept waving their bodies about in their saddles, thus disturbing the aim. A sturdy fight began and lasted about an hour—sometimes one party retreating, and then the other. But the savages soon found out that

Chapter Six · 97

they had not Mexican carbines to deal with, but Yankee rifles; and they fled the field, leaving all their animals and about a dozen prisoners, together with over twenty of their warriors slain. These showed real muscular power and handsome forms—but the savage was apparent in every part. Our men received many arrows in their clothes, but were all uninjured, except the Captain, who had two slight arrow wounds on the chin. A Mexican distinguished himself here by his skillful use of the lasso, having, with it, dragged down and killed two of the Indians. This is a terrible weapon in an experienced hand; and I have since heard that, among the forces sent out to meet us at Santa Fé, there were about one thousand lassoers. I would much rather encounter a Mexican armed with a carbine, than one holding a lasso. We had a man very badly injured, a short time after the period I am referring to, while away from camp. He was caught by a mounted Mexican in this way, and dragged some distance, tearing his face very much; but, luckily, the lasso did not go down low enough to entirely secure his arms, and he succeeded in freeing himself.

It was singular to see our men, who had come to make war on the Mexicans, turning round, and, at the hazard of their lives, protecting the property of the owner of El Poso. The latter generously presented each of his defenders with the horse he had ridden from Parras. Among the Indians slain, was their medicine-man, whose head our physician slily boar away for the sake of his skull. I heard that the mess to which the physician belonged, snuffed something occasionally that was not lavender, and it afterwards became a savage question among them, whether our man of medicine had sufficiently cured the cranium of the medicine-man to save it from Hamlet's remark on the skull of Yorick.

On entering the pretty town of Parras, we encamped in the Alameda. Here, General Wool had encamped for some time. The Alcalde told us that we must be very careful, or the Mexicans would steal everything from us—that General Wool, who was a Catholic, had very wrongly allowed them to thieve and abuse his men

98 · A Campaign in New Mexico

without giving the soldiers any redress. Our officers assured him that they would have rather different folks to deal with now. We were not five minutes in camp, before a thief got so beaten and kicked as to be hardly able to drag himself away.

The next day, a horrible occurrence took place. One of our cannon drivers, a young and remarkably inoffensive man, who had been on the sick list for a week previous, had started, with two or three companions, to take a look at the town; but, after proceeding some way, he had found himself too weak to go further, and had separated from his companions to return to camp, when a thorn having entered his foot, he drew off his boot and sat down in the street. He was looking into his boot, when a stone struck him on the forehead, and knocked him down senseless. He supposed that the Mexicans then beat him on the face with stones, and left him for dead. On recovering his senses, he made his way down to camp; and I never saw a more horrible sight than his face presented; his forehead was broken through in two places, and the flesh all cut to pieces, and his lower jaw broken; besides, a fracture just below the eye. His wounds were dressed, and he seemed to be rapidly recovering at the time we left him at Saltillo; but I afterwards heard that he died of lockjaw. The sight of our friend's bloody figure at once excited some of the soldiers; and they sallied into the town, and closed most of the shops. Vengeance was sworn, and each felt that, after what had happened, it would not require much provocation to produce an outbreak. Nor did it. A short time afterwards, a Mexican sat down on the pole of one of our wagons. The driver, who was sitting near, and who, from having been a prisoner among them for some time, spoke Spanish, told him, mildly, to get off, as the hounds were broken, and he was injuring the wagon by sitting on that part. The fellow insolently responded: "I shall not—this ground is as much mine as yours." Without another word, the teamster caught up his heavy iron-shod whip, and struck the Mexican on the left temple, fracturing the skull over four inches. He fell, but got up and staggered off.

CHAPTER SIX • 99

However, he died the same night. This occurrence happened before the house of the constable of the alcalde, who came running out with his staff of office in one hand, and a drawn sabre in the other, crying out, "Respect the law." But an American, standing by, knocked the constable down with his fist, and, seizing his sabre, bent it up and threw it into the sako. The constable moved off, and did not venture to interfere in that or any other matter during the day. In the night, a Mexican was found dead, with a horrible sabre wound in his breast, lying in the street.

This system of retaliation cannot be defended; but the offence on the Mexican side was very gross, after the uniform kind treatment they had met with from us; and it was more surprising, because this was the town where, when General Wool arrived, the inhabitants had quarreled as to who should receive and attend on the American sick—everybody being desirous to receive them into their houses. And we had never met with such treatment north of this place, the Mexicans seeming properly to appreciate the forbearance exhibited by our soldiers. Whenever we encamped, in five minutes, women and children would roam through the tents to sell different articles, never meeting with insult or injury.

Although we had flogged several Mexicans very severely at Chihuahua for stealing, yet the rest of the inhabitants were not dissatisfied; it being known that we were whipping common thieves, and that the example would, probably, prove beneficial.

CHAPTER SEVEN

WE HERE received orders to proceed southward; and after resting two days, again moved on. Looking back on Parras, the scene was beautiful; interspersed, as it was, with palms, lemon trees and vineyards. A short distance from this town is a large hacienda, which the owner is trying to arrange in American style. Thoughts of home were awakened by the sight of the first peaked roof that we had seen since we left Missouri.

On the twentieth we encamped at San Juan, the scene of a battle between Santa Anna and the Spaniards, during their revolution, as well as of a skirmish between a part of Taylor's force and the Mexicans.

The next day we pitched our tents at Encantada, half a mile from the battle-field of Buena Vista; and found a regiment of Arkansas cavalry encamped on the field. The next day a question, which had been frequently agitated in our camp, *Was there really such a man as General Wool?* (for we had gone some two thousand miles wool-gathering), was to be satisfied: he having now sent us word that he should review us the next day. We were certainly to have seen him at El Poso; we were positively to have aided him in the taking of Chihuahua: and he was most undoubtedly to receive us at Parras!

But now, we *had* unearthed our game; General Wool was certainly encamped only six miles off, in the direction of Saltillo. Some of us took the opportunity of going over the battle-field of Buena Vista; and it well repaid the trouble. The American position, un-

101

der the hills upon which Santa Anna had posted his artillery, was sufficiently marked by the ploughed-up ground, caused by the Mexican cannon-shot, and by marks of what had been pools of blood. It must have been a dreadful struggle. Remnants of uniform were strewed around, and one of my companions picked up a half of one of Santa Anna's forty-two pound shells. I have understood that all the Mexican shells burst exactly in halves, which was on account of the bad powder used to fill them; the service of a shell being, of course, increased according to the smallness of the fragments into which it splits. The half we found could not have been fractured more evenly with tools. On one part of the field is a long row of stones, I believe some three hundred in number, laid at the side of a trench in which the dead Mexicans were buried by their countrymen; and so slightly are they covered, that here an arm sticks out and there a leg. A stone was placed for each body deposited in the trench. I deem it unnecessary to give a description of the field; and would only remark upon the falsehood of Santa Anna's statement, that his army had been without food and water for forty-eight hours previous to, and during this battle; for one of his generals has since published a statement showing that he had several hundred head of beef-cattle, while a fine stream of water runs directly through the battle-ground.

The next day, the twenty-second of May, General Wool came over with his staff, in full uniform, and a guard of honor. After a formal review, he decided to keep our American battery of six pieces, but arranged that we should take the Mexican guns home. The next morning, as we passed his camp, the artillery company marched into it to deliver the guns; and General Wool made many complimentary remarks, and, among others, gave us to understand that we were covered with glory. This might be; but we were certainly not covered with it as with a garment. General Wool, turning to our major, remarked, that he should be very much pleased, indeed, to retain the company; but Major Clark told him that his boys had been too badly treated to wish to re-

CHAPTER SEVEN • 103

enlist. "But," returned Wool, "it shall be my endeavor to make them forget that, and I promise, if they will remain, they shall be treated in the best manner."

"That's what they told us when we started," gruffly responded the major. The general said no more.*

We passed through Saltillo the next day; and I was agreeably surprised to find it such a large and handsome place. The cathedral is beautiful, and most of the houses are high and ornamental. The inhabitants turned out to see us; and I beheld the prettiest girl I saw in all Mexico, standing at the door of a mean-looking dwelling in the main street. Her complexion, of marble whiteness, showed delicately a slight rosy color in the cheek, while her beautiful large dark swimming eyes, with their accompanying heavy lashes and eyebrows, rested with a pitying expression upon me— for I was lying at the time in a wagon on account of sickness. Oh the beauty of the exquisite Spanish word *pobrecito*, (poor fellow!) when heard from such lips—the sweetest of all sweet sounds.

The Mexican women in general are not handsome, for they commonly want the clear complexion, which we deem inseparable from beauty; but they have that large dark swimming eye, a lip usually high colored, and good teeth. But their principal charm lies in their manner. In entering a house, which you may do, even though a stranger, and be sure of a welcome from its owners, the senoras, without rising, offer you a seat, and are ready at once to converse with you on any subject, and this with a piquancy and naiveté exceedingly attractive to a foreigner. It is a pleasure to meet some pretty doña of your acquaintance after a short absence.

---

*Indeed, our treatment had been throughout very hard. Sometimes we were almost starved; and we did not recieve, except during the last month of our time, the full rations of food allowed by law to United States soldiers; and, on our arrival at New Orleans, our pay was also reduced a dollar a month, and we even then only received twelve and a half cents a day as commutation money for forage for our horses, during the time we received no corn from the government; whereas, I had frequently paid from fifty cents to seventy-five cents a day for my horse's provender.

104 · A Campaign in New Mexico

Wherever it may be, she immediately grasps your hand, draws you towards her, passes her arm round your waist, and presses you gently to her. This habit, of course, struck us at first as singular and rather forward, but the perfect *nonchalance* with which a lady friend will thus press you to her heart, perhaps every day, soon shows that it is, in reality, only a common kindly recognition. But the gusto and real grace with which two dirty old beggars will thus hug each other, is a singular sight. This mode of greeting is not confined to either sex.

The day before we arrived at General Wool's camp, we had polished up our American cannon so that we could see our bearded faces in them. While we lay there, a "regular" of Wool's army, (one of Washington's battery,) was examining them; while standing around were several of our men. "Why," said the regular, "these guns are quite new, a'n't they? You've never fired them, I suppose." This remark awakened the ire of one of our men, particularly as the regular calls himself a veteran, and looks down upon a ragged volunteer; and he tartly responded: "No, of course not; what do you think we found to fire at, you fool? But those pieces," pointing to our captured Mexican guns—"have been fired several times. By the by, Mr. Regular," added he, "what do you do with all the pieces you capture?" He of Washington's battery, completely crest-fallen, said, "we haven't captured any yet!" This the inquirer well knew, and also that, at Buena Vista, instead of taking any cannon, they had, in fact, lost three pieces. But the idea that any "regular" should not have heard of our gallant little battle, was rather annoying.

On the twenty-fifth, we encamped two miles from the celebrated Bishop's Palace, near Monterey. The capture of this massive stone building, which, from its position, was easily defensible, had proved a difficult and bloody undertaking, for, besides the building, there is a high stone enclosure, in front, which must have been carried only after a hard struggle. The edifice had, evidently, been a fine one; but it was now almost in ruins. The tremendous effect of artillery could here be observed. I remarked where a ball had entered the door, and, glancing off the side of the massive stair-case, had passed through, first a strong stone wall, which supplied the place of hand-rail, then through a partition wall, and then through the side of the house—the two last walls being of large stones, firmly cemented.

As we marched through Monterey, we passed, to our left, the cemetery in which Worth had placed his mortar, when bombarding the city. Monterey is beautifully situated in very rich valley; it is a place of considerable size, and has been a fine city. But the houses are very much cut up by musket and cannon ball. One of the principal public buildings, I understood it had been the custom-house, was completely destroyed in the siege. The wall surrounding the plaza is pierced at every short distance with port-holes, through which the inhabitants fired upon their assailants. The church itself bears numerous marks of balls. In front of the windows of all large houses in Mexico are gratings of iron, very often fancifully ornamented, and which form a cage about a foot deep round each window. In passing through the streets, many of these might be observed through which cannon balls had passed, cutting and twisting a gap through, perhaps, twenty bars; and there were many house-walls upon which a hand could not be placed without covering the mark of a musket ball. The Mexican houses are well adapted for a street fight, as, from the flat roofs above which the walls rise to a height of about two feet, a constant fire could be kept up without exposing any part of the person, while the streets, from being entirely unobstructed, present a clear sweep for the musketeer on the house-top.

We passed, on the road three miles beyond Monterey, the Black Fort, which had resisted Taylor in his attack on the city. At that time it was not finished, but has been since completed by the general's orders, and is rendered almost impregnable. It is advantageously situated, and there are many heavy guns mounted in it—among them are two very beautiful long "forty-two's," of English manufacture, several Spanish and many American pieces. There is one large gun with which the Mexicans attempted to

106 • A Campaign in New Mexico

send a shell to Taylor's camp at Walnut Springs, (three miles,) but putting in too much powder, the whole breech flew out and killed numbers of the sapient artillerists. There is also a Mexican piece, which, in one of the battles, received a ball directly in the muzzle, knocking out a large piece of the under-part of the mouth.

About noon we encamped at Walnut Springs. We saw nothing of old Rough and Ready for some hours afterwards, although we were near to the General's tent. In the afternoon, a rather common-looking man, dressed in a check shirt, fancy trowsers of common stuff, brown holland coat, and large straw hat, was observed examining our Mexican pieces of cannon very attentively; and it was soon whispered around, "that's him!" His whole appearance was such a contrast to Wool, for the latter came to our camp in full uniform, and in review style, that this unceremoniousness took us pleasantly by surprise. Many of our men, who had served with him in Florida, went up and shook hands with him, and were delighted to find he had remembered them. General Taylor hardly needs description now; and yet it is by no means an easy task to give it. His face, if it were not for the soul's expression there, would be considered far from handsome. But that simple, good and firm look which beams from his eyes is indescribable. In figure he is short, and—to use an ordinary but expressive phrase—stumpy, being inclined to *embonpoint;* and yet, when you hear him speak, you feel that a man not of the common mould stands before you. I was surprised to observe that his orderly servant was exactly the opposite in appearance to his officer, for although Taylor is by no means slovenly in his dress, yet there is a comfortable *abandon* about him that shows he takes no pride in dress:—while his orderly is the very pink of soldiers, being a young man of very fine form, and with long glossy black ringlets descending to his shoulders.

While we were at Walnut Springs, General Taylor addressed Colonel Doniphan thus: "By the by, Colonel, every one is talking of your charge at Sacramento. I understand it was a brilliant affair. I wish you would give me description of it, and of your manoevres."

CHAPTER SEVEN • 107

"Manoeuvres be hanged," returned Doniphan, and added, "I don't know anything about the charge, except that my boys kept coming to me to let them charge, but I would not permit them; for I was afraid they would all be cut to pieces. At last, I saw a favorable moment and told them they might go—they were off like a shot—and that's all I know about it!"

We left Walnut Springs about noon on the twenty-seventh of May, and continued our route to Camargo, where we were to take boat for a mouth of the Rio Grande. On the road we met with two thousand five hundred pack mules, carrying provisions for the army, on their way to Monterey. At sundown we encamped at Marin. General Taylor had ridden out with us two or three miles, and then, bidding us farewell in the kindest manner, returned to his camp.

The next day, we passed the place where the large train of wagons was burnt by Urrea's men, about the same time that the battle of Buena Vista was fought.

It was, indeed, even then a horrible sight to behold; and disgrace must ever attach to those officers having charge of the wagon-part of the quarter-master's department, who allowed the poor drivers to go unarmed, and the wagons to proceed with so exceedingly slight an escort. Every here and there were the burnt remains of wagons which the brutal Mexicans set fire to without unharnessing the mules from them, so that the frightened animals dashed off until they became wedged among the trees, where they were burnt with the wagons—and the bones of the slaughtered drivers were lying about in all directions. A spot was pointed out to me where one of the teamsters had been staked down, and then inhumanly butchered inch by inch;—others were burnt alive, and but few escaped.

A few steps from this scene, I beheld the dried-up body of a Mexican, who met his death under the following circumstances. An Arkansas cattle-driver had been to Monterey on business, and was returning with some soldiers who were carrying an express down to the mouth of the river; but the drover lagged behind some

108 · A Campaign in New Mexico

two or three hundred yards, when a Mexican shot at him from the side of the road. The ball fractured his thigh, and he fell from his horse. His assailant, thinking he was dead, jumped upon him, when the drover, drawing his pistol, shot him. The soldiers, returning on hearing the shots, left the Mexican to become the withered example I saw, and took the drover to Ceralvo, where his leg was amputated; and from this operation he was just recovering, when he caught the small-pox, and, at the time we passed through that place, was dying.

At this same Ceralvo we arrived on the twenty-ninth. It is one of the few places which Taylor did not destroy along the road:— he had been compelled to lay waste most of the ranchos and small towns, on account of their affording concealment to parties of guerrillas who would occasionally rob the wagon trains. We only halted here a few hours to rest, intending to proceed fifteen miles further in the cool of the afternoon. The heat had now become so excessive as to render it almost impossible to march in the middle of the day.

Taking a stroll through the town of Ceralvo, I found, sitting under a tree, dealing monte, a genuine specimen of the Texian ranger. His name, he said, was John Smith—a name which I thought I had heard before. In height he was about six feet four inches, of a stout sinewy frame, dressed in a mongrel attire, his coat being of American manufacture, his pantaloons Mexican, and his belt Indian. A fine white shirt, open some distance down, tied with a black silk handkerchief, studiedly knotted, and a Mexican sombrero, completed his dress. By his side was standing his younger brother, about fifteen years old, dressed, with little variation, in the same style, and with two enormous silver-mounted holster pistols in his waist, one under each arm. The elder also had a quantity of silver buttons and little ornaments upon his hatband and clothes; while, on the faces of both, the word desperado was indelibly stamped. I sat down by John Smith and drew him into conversation. He told me that the United States did not give the

CHAPTER SEVEN • 109

rangers any rations either for man or horse, but paid an equivalent; and that they procured their subsistence out of the Mexican's. And the process of doing this he thus graphically described: "Waal, you see when we want anything, a few of us start off to some rich hacienda near here, and tell the proprietor that in half an hour we must have so much of provisions. Waal, of course he don't like that much, so he refuses. One of us then just knots a lasso round the old devil's neck, and fastens it to his saddlebow, first passing it over a limb of some tree; then mounting his horse he starts off a few feet giving him a hoist, and then returns dropping him down again. After a few such swings, he soon provides what we have called for. Perhaps you think we've done with him then, eh? Not by a long shot. We have to jerk him a few times more, and then the money or gold-dust is handed out. When we've got everything out of him we let the yellow devil go. We don't hurt him much, and he soon gets over it." Who can wonder at the Mexican becoming a guerilla?

I have been credibly informed that when these rangers are sent out on scouting parties, a Mexican guide is generally provided, but that he never returns; the Texians always shooting him on some pretext or other before he gets back. Their usual mode is to frighten him with threats, and, after putting him under guard, to have one of their number go up to the poor fellow, and advise him to run off immediately, he sees the sentinel's back is turned. This he does, and the sentinel, having received his cue, shoots him while attempting to escape. One of the most dastardly acts I ever heard of was perpetrated by half a dozen Texian officers a short time before we came down. They had lost their way, and hired a Mexican to show them to their camp, which he faithfully performed; but when they came in sight of it, they drew lots who should shoot their faithful and unsuspecting guide—the one on whom the lot fell, immediately drew a pistol and shot him.

Most of these rangers are men who have been either prisoners in Mexico, or, in some way, injured by Mexicans, and they, there-

110 • A Campaign in New Mexico

fore, spare none, but shoot down every one they meet. It is said that the bushes, skirting the road from Monterey southward, are strewed with skeletons of Mexicans sacrificed by these desperadoes.

While we rested at Ceralvo, I witnessed the execution of a Mexican supposed to be one of Urrea's lawless band. The Texians pretended to consider him as such; but there was no doubt that this was only used as a cloak to cover their insatiable desire to destroy those they so bitterly hate. A furlough was found upon this Mexican, from his army, to visit his family, ending as our furloughs do, that should he overstay his leave of absence, he would be considered a deserter. This time he had considerably overstayed; and he himself stated that he had never intended to return, being in favor of the Americans. But the rangers tried him by a court-martial; and adjudged him to be shot that very day. As the hour struck, he was led into the public plaza; and five rangers took their post a few feet off, as executioners. The condemned coolly pulled out his flint and steel, and little paper-cigarito; and, striking a light, commenced smoking as calmly as can possibly be imagined, and—in two minutes—fell a corpse, with the still smoking cigarito yet between his lips. I did not see a muscle of his face quiver, when the rifles were levelled at him, but he looked coolly at his executioners, pressing a small cross, which hung to his neck, firmly against his breast. I turned from the scene sickened at heart.

This habit is universal among the Mexicans of both sexes of wearing around the neck a medal or cross, usually suspended by a small rosary. The medals, which are of brass and of English manufacture, often bear the figure and name of the patron saint of the wearer, but most of them are stamped with the form and name of "The Lady of Guadalupe"—of whom many miraculous tales are told; and on the reverse of the medal is the inscription, *Non fecit taliter ominationii*, which a late writer on Mexico translates, wittily, *She never made such a fool of any other nation.* The crosses are often of silver or gold. The love of ornaments and false jewelry among the lower orders of the Mexicans is remarkable. Every man and woman have their fingers loaded with common brass rights set with glass; and one of the most profitable articles of sale carried out by the traders, are the common gilt trinkets, usually styled Paris jewelry.

On the night of the thirtieth, we encamped at Mier, the scene of one of the bloodiest struggles of the Texian Revolution between the Texians, who had invaded the country, and the Mexican army. The buildings still stand in which General Green and his little band made such a desperate resistance against more than thrice their force, armed, too, with artillery. Now, in riding through the place, you find such signs as these: "Rough and Ready Eating House." "Hot Coffee and Cakes;"—"Taylor's Hotel. Good Segars."

We reached Camargo on the thirty-first; but found that the Rio Grande, which we here first saw again since leaving El Poso, was too low to allow steamboats to come up thus far—indeed, to me there was no perceptible difference in the appearance of the river, from what it was where we had left its banks, a thousand miles above. Camargo has now become a place of some importance, for, although there are but few substantial dwellings, yet there is quite a large number of canvas houses used for the protection of provisions and other stores landed from the steamboats, when the river is high, and sent hence in wagons to the army. These canvas houses are of immense extent, and stand in a cluster, surrounded by a trench and embankment. The River San Juan, which empties itself into the Rio Grande at this point, is ferried by means of flatboats guided by large ropes stretched from bank to bank.

We had brought several of the great traders' wagons down with us; and these immense machines, with their long ten-mule teams, proved a source of wonder and amusement to the teamsters who were here driving the United States wagons—they using moderate-sized light vehicles, drawn by only five mules. The latter are not so well adapted to this country as the large ones; and so thought the quarter-master stationed here, for he at once relieved us from most of our wagon-train, and tried to hire some of our old and experienced drivers for ten ten-mule teams, which he intended to put on the road at once. But, although he offered sixty dollars a month, and double rations, he could not procure a single hand, they having a great dislike to the regulars.

An attempt was also made by two of our officers, to induce some of us to re-enlist during the war, but this object could not be accomplished; we were *for going home to Sarah and the children!*— and for our pay, as even up to this point we had received none.

We marched but nine miles during the first morning we left Camargo; and before we reached our resting-place, we lost a man named Swain. He had very incautiously gone ahead of our advanced guard, some two or three hundred yards, and was riding through the muskeet bushes which skirt the road, and only a few paces from it, when he received a bullet in the back, killing him instantly. The advance guard pressed on, hearing the report, and caught sight of five mounted Spaniards going off at full speed. They chased them for some distance; but lost them on account of a deep gully which crossed their path. A few miles further, and we came to a town (the name of which I have forgotten), where we were to rest until the afternoon; and the guard, having observed that the Mexicans who had committed the outrage had taken this direction, searched the town, and found, at one house, five Mexicans, who evidently had just come off a journey, and also a like number of mules, the backs of which were yet wet from their saddles. On questioning the men, they said the mules did not belong to them, and that they had no saddles in the house; but, on searching, five were found, evidently only just removed from the backs of the mules. The Mexicans were at once arrested, and taken to the quarter-master who was stationed here. In spite of the evident guilt of the men, this officer said that he knew them, that they were in his employ, and that they could not be guilty. He removed them from our custody, and placed them in charge of his own guard. This incensed the messmates of poor Swain, and they vowed vengeance. Eight of them, mostly neighbors, at home, of

CHAPTER SEVEN • 113

his family, remained concealed behind us, and, as the quarter-master's guard escorted the suspected men out of the town, and turned them free, each Mexican received a rifle-ball, and never moved again. The avengers then proceeded to the house where the culprits had been found, and, after shooting two who were there, having since come in, burnt it to the ground, and quietly and coolly followed us.

News had been brought to us that five steamboats were lying at Reinosa; and several regiments, which had been discharged by Taylor, being also on the march for that place, we were obliged to push on as fast as possible, in order that we might get the first chance. This we did, and we managed to get ahead of all but one regiment, which was only a few hours' march before us; so it was resolved to push on all this night, in order to reach Reinosa by sunrise. At midnight, as we were moving as rapidly as possible, we came upon the above regiment encamped; and they, perceiving our object, at once struck tents, and came after us; but we had got too much the start of them, and they did not arrive at Renosa until after our officers had secured the only two available boats; three others being hard aground on the bar below the town, and the water falling fast.

In coming down the road, our men caught three armadillos. A soldier amused me one evening, by describing his encounter with one of these harmless creatures. It seems, he had gone among the bushes to shoot a deer which he had seen pass, when, as he said, an armadillo, the like of which he had never seen before, ran at him! (quite an improbability,) caused his mule to rear, and he, shooting the animal *instanter*, never stopped to examine it, but hurried back as fast as possible to the ranks.

The general appearance of the country has not been previously mentioned. The whole extent of what we had travelled through, except just along the banks of streams, is of the most barren description, being principally composed of a hard yellow clay, so poor that, in most places, grass cannot be raised. I have travelled more than a hundred miles at a time without seeing sufficient grass to furnish my horse with a meal, and without meeting with a stone as large as a pebble. The roads, except in a few places where they happen to cross mountains, are excellent, being as hard and level as a floor. The land can only be cultivated just along the banks of the streams; and there the fertility of the soil amply repays the farmer, as the crops do not seem to exhaust the ground. Many farmers work the same ground fifty years or more, without spreading upon it a particle of manure. The seasons are also favorable to the husbandman. Rain, however, is rare. Before we left El Poso, which was in January, the inhabitants were ploughing and sowing corn. I have no doubt that, were the Mexicans not so excessively lazy, they might produce anything they chose; but when they have put seed into the ground, they think they have done enough; and if it should not come up and the plant thrive, instead of doing as we should, setting to work to remedy it, they simply "call on Hercules;" in other words, fall upon their knees at the altar before the priest, tell him how unfortunate they have been, buy a blessing from him, and go home in blessedness. The inhabitants produce maize, wheat, oats, onions, melons, grapes and several other fruits. I never saw any potatoes, although, as we know, it is currently said that the root grows wild in the southern parts of Mexico. I have seen as fine melons, grapes and corn in Mexico as I have observed anywhere; and I have purchased onions as large as an ordinary sized dinner plate.

The first sight of the steamboat pipes on the Rio Grande was hailed by us with three cheers, for they were the first we had seen since we left Missouri, and we now felt sure we were getting towards home—and perhaps the feeling was increased with me, for it happened to be my birth-day. All the sick were put into the first boat the next morning. They numbered about one hundred and fifty, and then about as many more were crowded in. Our voyage lasted four days, we stopping every evening at sundown, when we would land to cook and sleep.

CHAPTER SEVEN • 115

The Rio Grande can never be considered a navigable river, for this it is not even for the very smallest steamboats higher up than Reinosa, except in extraordinary stages of water; and even in the few miles we sailed down it, we were almost all the time struggling over sand-bars, and the river was so crooked that there was hardly room for the boats to turn properly. The scarcity of wood along its bank will always be a drawback to its navigation; but still the little wood found is of the best quality, being mostly ebony and lignum vitae, which, from the great quantity of oil contained in them, make an intense fire. The windings of the Rio Grande are remarkable. There is one hacienda on its banks which a boat passes in front of seven times, after coming in sight of, and before actually reaching it;—the river making seven close convolutions east and west in perhaps twelve miles of country; and there is one of the turns where you pass a long low bank for five miles, and can look over and see the river again not one hundred feet from you on the other edge. Thus, after sailing in reality ten miles along, the voyager has actually only advanced two hundred yards south. The banks and channels of the river are continually changing, and the sand of which the former are wholly composed, is constantly being washed down and filling up the bed of the river.

Colonel Doniphan here published an order from the Secretary of War, requiring him to detail ten men from each company to take the horses of the whole command to Missouri by the way of Texas; but a difficulty arose from an inability to find men willing to prolong their term of service, which had, in fact, already expired, because such a journey would occupy two months, whereas we might go at once to New Orleans in less than two weeks. At last, the affair was settled by a sergeant agreeing to take any number of the horses at five dollars a head; and he thus collected several hundred of them. The officers, whose duty it was to see to the shipping of the returned volunteers, notified us that, with the exception of blankets, arms and clothing, nothing would be transported for us, and we were thus reduced to the necessity of leaving our saddles and other things on the banks of the river. The equipments, thus about to be left, were looked at with wistful eyes by the lower order of Mexicans, so we piled them in a large heap and burnt them. All our extra blankets, buffalo robes, and everything we could spare, we cast upon the pile. I observed a Mexican knocked over by one of our men for offering him one dollar for his saddle, the latter declaring that a saddle which had carried a Missourian so many miles as his had, should not be sold to a Mexican for twenty dollars—and it was instantly committed to the flames.

We passed Matamoros on one side and Fort Brown on the other, but were not permitted to land. The next evening we encamped at the mouth of the river, and found there a New York regiment, waiting for a boat to take them up; and among the officers, I recognized old acquaintances, and heard home news. One of the officers desired to know from me, how we had fared? and when I had given him a few items, he thought it rather tough; "but," observed he, "we shall be treated better," adding, with a sneer, "we are not volunteers, we are regulars."

We lay encamped here until noon of the ninth of June, when we moved to Brazos Santiago. I believe that the position of this place is not properly understood. It is simply an island formed by a shallow arm of the sea, which is nearly dry at low tide on the western side, where the water is narrow which separates it from the projection of land forming the mouth of the river. On the north-east, across the strip of water, which is here of considerable depth, is Point Isabel, now the site of a fine hospital, being the only kind of building that should ever be permitted upon that barren sand bank, which has proved destructive to many brave soldiers. One regiment alone left three hundred, who had died there of fever. The island of Brazos is supposed to have been the site of one of the largest and richest of the ancient Mexican cities, but which was swallowed up by the sea.

Our embarkation for New Orleans was in two vessels, one of them a small bark, wherein myself and some three hundred and

CHAPTER SEVEN • 117

fifty companions were packed. Her hold, containing one hundred double berths, was in such a filthy condition that we preferred the desk as a sleeping-place, and it was a struggle with us who should get his blanket first on desk, as those who were crowded out were compelled to go below. We ran short of water, and began to think ourselves on a worse *jornada* than ever.

Oh! the relief felt after almost four thousand miles of rough travel,* as we reached New Orleans, and placed our feet once more upon American soil! We were still in our tattered clothes, with unshorn beards and without a cent in our pockets; but "Sarah and the children" were now not far off!

*See table of distances traversed, in the Appendix No. 4.

APPENDIX

No.I.—Semi-Official Report of the Battle of Bracito.

No.II.—Official Report of the Battle of Sacramento.

No.III.—Mexican Government Extra,
showing the American Force.

No.IV.—Table of Distances traversed.

APPENDIX

No.I.

SEMI-OFFICIAL REPORT OF THE
BATTLE OF BRACITO.

Detachment of Missouri Light Artillery.
Camp below Bracito, Rio Grande, Dec. 26, 1846.

DEAR SIR:—I can only write to you a few lines, being upon the point of breaking up camp. Our detachment overtook Col. Doniphan's command at Fra Cristobal. Major Gilpin, with 250 men, had previously left for El Poso, and Col. Jackson was following with 200 men. Col. Doniphan had but 150 men with him, the remainder of his regiment being sick, attending on sick, and detached through the country. From Fra Cristobal our detachment marched with Colonel Doniphan south. When at the Laguna of the jornada del Muerte, news reached us through an express sent by Major Gilpin that the Mexicans had determined to resist at El Poso, and had collected a considerable number of troops intending to give us battle. An express had been sent to Santa Fé for part of the artillery under Major Clark, but no news had as yet reached us from there, so that a detachment of 30 men from the three companies of our corps are all that are here from the battalion. At the southern end of the jornada, ten miles north of Dona Ana, the traders had encamped. Contradictory rumors of the enemy's approach reached us daily.

Yesterday (Christmas day), when we had just arrived in camp here with about 600 men, had unsaddled our animals, and most of the men engaged in carrying wood and water, the news was brought into camp of the enemy's being in sight and advancing. It was about 2 o'clock P.M., and the day was very pleasant. Our horses were grazing some distance from camp at the time; we formed a single line and determined to meet the enemy as infantry. Their attack being evidently designed on the left flank, near which was our wagon train, our detachment was ordered from the extreme right to the left, where we soon took up our position. One piece of artillery, 490 regular lancers and cavalry, and 100 regular infantry, besides some 500 militia troops from El Poso, composed the enemy's force, according to the best information I can obtain from reports of prisoners and from papers found among the baggage on the field of battle. The enemy ranged the mountains in their rear. In our rear was the river, with a little bush-wood on its banks.

Previous to the encounter, a lieutenant from their ranks came forward waving a black flag in his hand, but halted when within one hundred steps of our line. Thomas Caldwell, our interpreter, rode out to meet him. The messenger with the black flag of defiance demanded that the commander should come into their camp, and speak to their general. The reply was, "If your general wants to see our commander, let him come here." "We shall break your ranks, then, and take him there," was the retort of the Mexican. "Come and take him," said our interpreter, unwittingly using the phrase of the Spartan at Thermopylae. "A curse on you; prepare for a charge," cried the Mexican; "we give no quarters, and ask none;" and waving his black flag gracefully over his head, galloped back towards the enemy's line. Their charge was made by the dragoons from their right, directed upon our left flank, bringing our detachment into the closest fire. Their infantry with one howizter with them, at the same time attacking our right flank.

Their charge was a handsome one, but was too well, too coolly met, to break our line. After their fire had been spent, their front column being at about 100

No. 1 • 121

steps from the front of our flank, our line poured a volley into them, which being a few times repeated, created such havoc in their columns, that their forces wheeled to the left, retreating from our fire, and in their flight made an attack on the provision train. Here they met a very warm reception, and were soon compelled to fly in all directions, and in the utmost confusion. Their infantry having been put to flight, the Howard company, under the command of Lieut. N. Wright, taking advantage of the panic, charged upon them, and took their cannon from them. This was soon manned by the artillery detachment under Lieut. Kribben, in Col. Mitchell's escort. The enemy had by this time fled, leaving their arms, baggage, provisions and other stores, on the field of battle.

A small body of mounted men under the command of Capt. Reid, had by this time gathered together in a line, and charged upon the enemy, pursuing them into the mountains, where they sought refuge.

The number of their dead is said to be at least thirty; that of their wounded was slight, so far as ascertained. Had we had a single piece of cannon with us they would have lost more of their men; but having no artillery on our side, we had to act as infantry until we got possession of the howitzer so gallantly captured by the Howard company.

We lost not a single man, and had but seven slightly wounded. We took eight prisoners, six of whom died last night. Thus ended the battle of Bracito, the first battle of the Army of the West, and as bravely fought by our men as ever men fought at any engagement.

We have every reason to believe that there is more in store for us.

C.H. Kribben,
1st Lieut. Mo. Light Artillery.

122 • APPENDIX

No. II.

OFFICIAL REPORT OF THE
BATTLE OF SACRAMENTO.

SPECIAL DESPATCH FROM MAJOR M. LEWIS CLARK.

Headquarters, Battalion Missouri Light Artillery.
Camp near Chihuahua, Mexico, March 2, 1847.

To Col. A.W. Doniphan, Commanding American Forces
in the State of Chihuahua:—

SIR:—I have the honor to report, that, agreeably to your instructions, I left
the camp near *Sauz,* on the morning of the 28th ultimo, accompanied by my
Adjutant, Lieut. L.D. Walker, and non-commissioned staff, and proceeded in
advance to a position commanding a full view of the enemy's camp and entrenchments, situated about four miles distant from this point. The enemy was
discovered to be in force, awaiting our approach, having occupied the ridge and
neighboring heights about Sacramento. Upon examination, it was ascertained
that his entrenchments and redoubts occupied the brow of an elevation extending across the ridge between the *Arroyo Seco* and that of *Sacramento*—both of
which, at this point, cross the valley from the elevated ridge of mountains in the
rear of the village of *Torreon,* known by the name of the *Sierra de Victoriano,* that
of *Nombre de Dios* on the east, and through which runs the *Rio del Nombre de
Dios.* This valley is about four miles in width, and entrenched by the enemy
entirely across, from mountain to mountain, the road to the city of Chihuahua
running directly through its centre—and of necessity passing near to, and crossing the *Rio Sacramento,* at the *Rancho Sacramento,* a strongly built and fortified
house, with adjoining corraals, and at other enclosures, belonging to Angel Trias,
the Governor of Chihuahua. From observation, it was ascertained that the enemy had occupied the site between these hills, and that the batteries upon them
were supported by infantry—his cavalry being in advanced positions, formed
into three columns, between the *Arroyo Seco,* and our advance. During these
observations, the enemy's advance guard discovering my party, approached rapidly, with the evident intention of intercepting it, but being met by that of our
troops, which I had sent forward, it as rapidly retreated. At this time, also, the

three columns of the enemy's cavalry recrossed the *Arroyo Seco,* and retired behind their entrenchments. I then approached within six hundred yards of the most advanced redoubt, from which point the enemy's formation was plainly discernible. The entrenchments consisted of a line with intervals composed of circular redoubts, from three to five hundred yards interval, with entrenchments between each, covering batteries partly masked by cavalry. The redoubt nearest to my position, contained two pieces of cannon, supported by several hundred infantry.

The enemy's right and left were strong positions—the *Cerro Frijoles* on his right, and having high precipitous sides, with a redoubt commanding the surrounding country, and the pass leading towards Chihuahua, through the Arroyo Seco. The Cerro Sacramento on his left, consisting of a pile of immense volcanic rocks, surmounted by a battery, commanded the main road to Chihuahua, leading directly in front of the enemy's entrenchments; crossing the Rio Sacramento at the rancho, directly under its fire, and also commanding the road from Terreon, immediately in its rear; the crossing of the main road over the Arroyo Seco, at the point from which my reconnaissance was made, laid directly under the fire of the batteries on the enemy's right, which rendered it necessary to ascertain the practicability of a route more distant from the enemy's entrenchments. The passage was found to be practicable, with some little labor, and a point selected as the best for the passage of the artillery, and wagons, and merchants' trains. The whole point of the enemy's line of entrenchments appeared to be about two miles, and his force 3000 men. The artillery being masked, the number and calibre of the cannon could not be estimated.

Further, I have the honor to report, that the battalion of artillery under my command, composed of 110 men, and seven officers, with a battery of six pieces of artillery, were, on the morning of the battle, directed to form, under the direction of Capt. Weightman, between the two columns of merchants' and provision wagons; being thus masked from the view of the enemy. In this column my troops continued the march to within fifteen hundred yards of the enemy's most advanced position; our direction was then changed to the right, and the column having crossed the Arroyo Seco without reach of the enemy's fire, rapidly advanced towards the table land between the Seco and Sacramento. At this time the enemy was perceived advancing from his entrenchments, to prevent our seizing upon the heights, but by a rapid movement of the battery, it was quickly drawn from its mask, and seizing upon a favorable position, protected in the rear by a mask, from the attack of a large body of the enemy's cavalry, ascertained to be hanging on our rear, it was formed, and at once opened

124 • APPENDIX

fire upon the enemy's cavalry, rapidly advancing upon us. At this time his charging column was about 900 yards distant, and the effect of our strap shot and shells was such as to break his ranks and throw his cavalry into confusion. The enemy now rapidly deployed into line, bringing up his artillery from the entrenchments. During this time our line was preparing for a charge—my artillery advancing by hand and firing. The enemy now opened a heavy fire of cannon upon our line, mainly directed upon the battery, with little effect. Lieutenant Dorn had his horse shot under him by a nine pound ball, at this stage of the action, and several mules and oxen in the merchant wagons, in our rear, were wounded or killed, which, however, was the only damage done.—The fire of our cannon at this time, had such good effect, as to dismount one of the enemy's pieces, and completely to disperse his cavalry, and drive him from his position, forcing him to again retire behind his entrenchments. For a short time, the firing on either side now ceased, and the enemy appeared to be removing his cannon and wounded, whilst our line prepared to change our position, and more towards the right, for the purpose of occupying a more advantageous ground. Our object being soon gained, the order to advance was given, and immediately after I was directed to send the section of howitzers, to support a charge upon the enemy's left. I immediately ordered Captain R.H. Weightman to detach the section, composed of two 12 pound mountain howitzers, mounted upon carriages constructed especially for field prairie service, and drawn by two horses each. These were commanded by Lieutenants E.F. Chouteau and H.D. Evans, and manned by some twenty men, whose conduct in this action cannot be too much commended.

Captain Weightman charged at full gallop upon the enemy's left, preceded by Captain Reid and his company of horse, and after crossing a ravine some hundred and fifty yards from the enemy, he unlimbered the guns within fifty yards of the entrenchment, and poured a destructive fire of canister into his ranks, which was warmly returned, but without effect. Capt. Weightman again advanced upon the entrenchments, passing through it in the face of the enemy, and within a few feet of the ditches; and in the midst of crossfires from three directions, again opened his fire, to the right and left with such effect, that with the formidable charge of the cavalry and dismounted men to your own regiment, and Lieutenant Col. Mitchell's escort, the enemy were driven from the breastworks on our right in great confusion. At this time, under a heavy crossfire from a battery of four six pounders, under Lieuts. Dorn, Kibben, and Labeaume, upon the enemy's right, supported by Major Gilpin on the left, and the wagon train escorted by two companies of infantry under Captains E.F.

No. II · 125

Glasgow, and Skillman in the rear, Major Gilpin charged upon the enemy's centre and forced him from his entrenchments under a heavy fire of artillery, and small arms. At the same time, the fire of our own battery was opened upon the enemy's extreme right, from which a continued fire had been kept up upon our line and the wagon train. Two of the enemy's guns were now soon dismounted on their right, that battery silenced, and the enemy dislodged from the redoubt, on the *Cerro Frijoles*. Perceiving a body of lancers forming, for the purpose of outflanking our left, and attacking the merchant train under Captain Glasgow, I again opened upon them a very destructive fire of grape and spherical case shot, which soon cleared the left of our line. The enemy vacating his entrenchments and deserting his guns, was hotly pursued towards the mountains beyond Cerro Frijoles, and down *Arroyo Seco de Sacramento,* by both wings of the army, under Lieutenant Col. Mitchell, Lieutenant Col. Jackson, and Major Gilpin, and by Captain Weightman, with the section of howitzers. During this pursuit, my officers repeatedly opened their fires upon the retreating enemy with great effect. To cover this flight of the enemy's forces from the entrenched camp, the heaviest of his canon had been taken from the entrenchments to the *Cerro Sacramento,* and a heavy fire opened upon our pursuing forces and the wagons following in the rear. To silence this battery, I had the honor to anticipate your order to that effect, by at once occupying the nearest of the enemy's entrenchments, 1225 yards distant, and notwithstanding the elevated position of the Mexican battery, giving him a plunging fire into my entrenchments, which was not defiladed, and the greater range of his long nine-pounders, the first fire of our guns dismounted one of his largest pieces, and the fire was kept up with such briskness and precision of aim, that the battery was soon silenced, and the enemy seen precipitately retreating. The fire was then continued upon the Rancho Sacramento, and the enemy's ammunition and wagon-train retreating upon the road to Chihuahua. By their fire, the house and several wagons were rendered untenable and useless. By this time, Lieutenant Colonel Mitchell had scaled the hill, followed by the section of howitzers, under Captain Weightman, and the last position of the Mexican forces was taken possession of, by our troops; thus leaving the American forces masters of the field. Having silenced the fire from Cerro Sacramento, one battery was removed into the plain at the rancho, where we gained the road, and were in pursuit of the enemy, when I received your order to return and encamp within the enemy's entrenchments for the night. From the time of first opening my fire upon the Mexican cavalry, to the cessation of the firing upon the rancho and battery of Sacramento, was about three hours, and during the whole time of the action, I take the utmost pleasure in stating, that every officer and man of my command, did his duty with cheerfulness, coolness, and precision, which is sufficiently shown by the admirable effect produced by their fire, the great accuracy of their aim, their expedition and ingenuity in supplying deficiencies in the field during the action, and the prompt management of their pieces—rendered still more remarkable, from the fact, that I had, during the fight, less than two-thirds the number of cannoniers generally required for the service of light artillery, and but four of the twelve artillery carriages belonging to my battery harnessed with horses, the remaining eight carriages being harnessed to the mules of the country. During the day my staff were of the greatest service—Adjutant Leo. D. Walker having been sent with the howitzers, and the non-commissioned officers remaining with me, to assist in the service of the battery. In this action, the troops under your command have captured one nine-pounder mounted on a cheek trail carriage, one nine-pounder, one six-pounder, and seven four-pounder guns, all mounted on new stock-trail carriages. These pieces were manufactured in Chihuahua, except the six pounder, which is an old Spanish piece. Three of the four-pounders were made at the mint in Chihuahua. Seven of the ten pieces were spiked, but have been unspiked since their capture; four of these were rendered unserviceable in the action; one entirely dismounted, was seized by my Adjutant, whilst in the act of being dragged from the field by the retreating enemy. There were also taken, two pieces of artillery, mounting three wall pieces of one and a half inch calibre each, and these are formidable weapons upon a charging force. With these twelve pieces of artillery was taken a due proportion of ammunition, implements, harness, mules, &c.; and they may be rendered serviceable by being properly repaired and manned; for which purpose I would ask for further reinforcement of my command. It is with feeling of gratitude to the Ruler of all battles, that I have now the honor to report, that not a man of my command has been hurt, nor any animals, with the exception of one horse killed under Lieutenant Dorn, chief of the first section of six-pound guns, and of one mule, belonging to the United States, shot under one of the cannoniers; neither has a gun or other carriage of my battery been touched, except in one instance, when a nine pound ball struck the tire of a wheel, without producing injury. This is a fact worthy of notice, that so little damage was done to a command greatly exposed to the enemy's fire, and of itself made a point of attack by the enemy, if I may so judge by the showers of cannon and other shot constantly poured into us, as long as the enemy continued to occupy his position. I might call your

No. III · 127

attention to the individual instances of personal courage and good conduct of the men of my command, as well as of the intrepid bravery, cool and determined courage of many of your own regiment, and Lieutenant Col. Mitchell's escort, who charged with us upon the enemy's works, were it not impossible, in any reasonable space, to name so many, equally worthy of distinction; and did I not presume that other field officers on that occasion, would report the proceedings of their own commands, and the praiseworthy conduct of their own officers and men.

With high respect,

I am, Sir, Your Most

Obedient Servant,

M. LEWIS CLARK,

Major Commanding Bat. Mo. Light Artillery.

No. III.

ALCANCE, AL FARO, NUMERO 14.

Chihuahua, Febrero 17 de 1847.

By a courier which arrived last evening at this capital we have the following news.

On the 9th inst. the invasive forces which occupied the city of El Paso, passed by San Elecario in the direction of this capital.—Since the 5th inst. their vanguard, composed of one hundred men, under the command of Col. Mitchell, have already occupied this fort (S. Elecario). The rest of the force, forming the centre and the reserve, amounts to seven hundred and seventy men, besides seventy-four wagons, which precede as many more wagons, loaded with munitions of war and provisions. Their artillery consists of four pieces of six pounds, two eight pounders, the obus which they took at Temascalitos, and a little mortar for stones which they obtained at San Elecario, after having committed many outrages and violences there. They also bring a wagon with the arms which they took from the suburbs of El Paso, and those which our troops left there in their retreat; their horses and oxen are in very bad condition.

The fear which possesses the soldiers is well known, since they themselves say that they come against their will, and this is proved, by the desertion of several of them; and by the questions which all ask, if any troops have come

128 · APPENDIX

from Mexico to Chihuahua, and whether they have cannon. They also intend carrying with them as prisoners, the priest of El Paso, the prefect Don R. Barela, and some other persons of distinction, considering them as a guarantee against any rebellion which the Pasénians may intend, or as hostages should such an event occur.

On the 7th inst. there came to them a courier with the news that the *so called Governor* of New Mexico, Charles Bent, Esq., and fifteen soldiers of his guard had been assassinated by the New Mexicans, and that all that State is following in an arduous insurrection, which has been promoted principally by the people of the Upper river. On account of this news they find themselves undecided what course to pursue, but Kirker has stimulated them to advance, telling them that Chihuahua will not be able to present in resistance, a force of more than 1000 men, militia and citizens, and commanded by poor officers. And he has made them believe that he gives their service the preference over the war with the Apaches for us, and the pay for which is still owing to him.

The arms which part of these soldiers which they call Mounted Dragoons carry, is a rifled musket with a bayonet, and a six barreled pistol in the cartridge box belt; the other part which they wish to consider as a light cavalry, use a shorter rifle, with sabre and six shooter at the belt. All their animals are in very bad order, and most of the soldiers are mounted on mules. A certain Owens and a Spaniard named Don Manuel (Harmony) have offered them resources of money when they occupy this capital.

No. IV.

TABLE OF DISTANCES TRAVERSED.

1846		MILES	
June 30.	Fort Leavenworth to Eleven mile Creek,	11	
July 1.	Eleven mile Creek to Rock Creek,	15	26
2.	Rock Creek to Kansas River,	10	36
3.	Camp (waiting for train).		
4.	Kansas River to Elm Grove,	20	56
5.	Elm Grove to One hundred and ten mile Creek,	22	78
6.	To above Rock Creek,	21	99

No. IV · 129

7.	Rock Creek to East of Big St. John's Spring,	23	122
8.	Big St. John's Spring to Diamond Spring,	22	144
9.	Diamond Spring to Cotton-Wood Fork,	24	168
10.	In camp (rain).		
11.	Cotton-wood Fork to Turkey Creek,	29	197
12.	Turkey Creek to Little Arkansas River,	25	222
13.	Little Arkansas to Cow Creek,	23	245
14.	Cow Creek to Arkansas Bend,	22	267
15.	Arkansas Bend to Pawnee Fork,	35	302
16.	In camp on account of high water.		
17.	Pawnee Fork to Coon Creek,	16	318
18.	Arkansas Coon Creek to Arkansas River,	25	343
19.	Along the Arkansas River,	24	367
20.	do	23	390
21.	do	13	403
22.	do to crossings,	23	426
23.	do	20	446
24.	do	22	468
25.	do	22	490
26.	do	19	509
27.	Along the Arkansas River to Big Timber,	20	529
28.	do	18	547
29.	do to mouth Piquetway Creek,	15	562
30 to Aug. 1.	In camp twelve miles below Bent's Fort.		
Aug. 2.	To Timpa Creek (west of Arkansas),	39	601
3.	To another camp on same creek,	7	608
4.	To Hole in the Rock,	23	631
5.	To Piquetway Fork,	30	661
6.	To foot of the Ratone Mountains,	7	668
7.	Within the Ratone Mountains,	15	683
8.	To Rio Colorado (Canadian North Fork),	16	699
9.	In camp (resting animals).		
10.	To Rio Bermejo,	22	721
11.	To Rion (near Ponia),	20	741
12.	To Ocaté,	22	763
13.	To lower Moro Settlements,	29	792
14.	To Las Begas,	17	809

130 • APPENDIX

15.	To first San Miguel Settlements (Tocolote),	18	827
16.	To Susano,	18	845
17.	To Pecos (ruins and rancho),	17	862
18.	Santa Fé,	28	890

Measurement of Lieut. Emory of Topographical Engineers   883

SANTA FÉ TO EL PASO.

1846

Dec. 6.*	Santa Fé to La Mayada,	35	
7.	To Bernalillo,	15	50
8.	To Ranchos de Albuquerque,	19	69
9.	To San Fernando,	20	89
10.	To Belen (cross river),	9	98
11.	To Sabinal,	12	110
12.	To opposite La Joya de Cibollita,	9	119
13.	To El Imitar,	6	125
14.	To Islopez (last settlement),	10	135
15.	To Cotton-wood camp on Rio Grande,	12	147
16.	To Valverde ruins (cross river),	10	157
17.	To Camp Cantadero (overtake Colonel Doniphan), 6		163
18.	To Camp Fra Christobal,	6	169
19.	To Camp Sierrita (on Jornada del Muerto),	18	187
20.	To Aleman (do)	24	211
21.	To Camp San Diego (do)	24	235
22.	To Roblero on Rio Grande,	12	247
23.	To Campos de Dona Ana	12	259
24.	To Dead man's Camp,	10	269
25.	To Temascalitos (battle of Bracito),	15	284
26.	To Lagunita,	16	300
27.	To El Paso del Norte (cross river),	20	320

*Not the route mentioned in the narrative, being down the east bank instead of crossing at Albuquerque.

No. IV · 131

EL PASO TO CHIHUAHUA.

1847

Feb. 5.	From El Paso to Presidio de San Elecario,	25	345
to 10.	In camp.		
11.	To Camp Alarm,	12	357
12.	To " Cumanche,	11	368
13.	In "		
14.	To " on jornada de Cantadero	18	386
15.	To " do	22	408
16.	To Lago de los Patos,	20	428
17.	In camp waiting for train.		
18.	To " near Carrizal,	15	443
19.	In "		
20.	To " Ravine (near Ojo Caliente),	6	449
21.	To " Jesus Maria (on Jornada de J.M.),	21	470
22.	To " Chivata do	20	490
23.	To " Galleguito,	12	502
24.	To Camp on Jornada Chicita,	10	512
25.	To " Laguna de encenillas,	15	527
26.	To Rancho Penol,	22	549
27.	To " Sauze,	13	562
28.	To " Sacramento (battle),	19	581
March 1.	To beyond Sacramento River,	4	585
2.	To City of Chihuahua,	16	501

CHIHUAHUA TO BRAZOS SANTIAGO.

1847.

April 25.	Chihuahua to Marble Ranch,	6	
26.	To Bachiniber,	29	35
27.	To Santa Cruz,	25	60
28.	In camp.		
29.	Santa Cruz to Saucillo,	24	84
30.	Saucillo to San Rosalia,	29	113
May 1.	In camp.		
2.	San Rosalia to Rancho Remada,	23	136
3.	To Guajaquilla,	32	168

4.	To Camp Cajote (on Jornada),	19	187
5.	To " San Berrado,	42	229
6.	To " El Andaboso,	12	241
7.	To Fort Pelayo,	25	266
8.	To Rancho Cadena,	18	284
9.	To Mapimi,	21	305
10.	To San Sebastiano,	37	342
11.	To San Lorenzo,	25	367
12.	To Juan Baptista,	17	384
13.	To El Paso (Indian skirmish),	25	409
14.	To Parras,	25	434
15 and 16.	In camp.		
17.	From Parras to Rancho Cienega,	26	460
18.	To Rancho Castamula,	17	477
19.	To " Vacarilla,	27	504
20.	To San Juan (former battle field),	21	525
21.	To Encantada (Buena Vista),	10	535
22.	In camp.		
23.	From Buena Vista through Saltillo to Rancho de los Gonzales	17	552
24.	To Rinconada,	28	580
25.	To Santa Catarina,	30	610
26.	To General Taylor's camp below Monterey,	9	619
27.	To Marin,	21	640
28.	To Rancho Viejo,	32	672
29.	To Punto Aguela,	22	694
30.	To Mier,	28	722
31.	To Camargo,	25	747
June 1.	To Reinosa,	48	795
2.	In camp waiting for boat.		
3.	Embark on steamboat J.F. Roberts.		
4.	To Matamoros by boat,	50	845
5.	To mouth of Rio Grande, do	27	872
6 to 8.	In camp.		
9.	To Brazos Santiago on foot,	6	878

No. I · 133

TOTAL AMOUNT IN MILES OF OUR WHOLE ROUTE.

St. Louis, Missouri, to Fort Leavenworth, by boat,	330
Fort Leavenworth to Santa Fé,	886
Santa Fé to Tomae and back,	190
Santa Fé to San Ildefonso and back,	120
Santa Fé to El Paso,	320
El Paso to Chihuahua,	280
Chihuahua to San Pablo and back,	120
Chihuahua to Brazos Santiago,	878
Brazos to New Orleans, by boat,	800
New Orleans to St. Louis,	1200
Total	5124 miles.

THE END.

Chapter Abstracts

Chapter One

Texas and her boundary. Army of the West and the author's volunteering at St. Louis. A *coup d'oeil*. The prairies. Indian woman and her child. A rain-storm. The son of the murdered Chavis. Swarm of annoying insects. Buffaloes and buffalo meat. Fish in the prairies. A volunteer buried. Sand-hills and their appearance owing to sunlight. Gusts of hot wind. Wolves. A volunteer in a fit likely to have been shot. Indian fear of cannon. Dead Indian chief in a tree. The dried body of an Indian walking. Prairie-dog towns and rattlesnakes.

Chapter Two

Rendezvous of the army near Bent's Fort. Soldiers put on short allowance. Slapjacks. Number of troops. A suspicous Mexican shown the camp and dismissed. Hunters. Antonio, his lasso and silver mounted saddle. The Rocky Mountains. A thunder storm. First Mexican settlement. Expected fight. Son of General Salazar taken. San Miguel del Vada. Pecos, an Aztec town, and its traditions and immense bones. A Catholic mule. Santa Fé, its palace and its calaboose. Shops for the traders. Kendall's gun. Burying Mexican children. Inhabitants described. Jars. Tortillas and Atole. Donkeys. Mules and their title deeds. Mustangs and a particular cream colored stallion. Mode of breaking the wild horse.

135

CHAPTER THREE

Ugly old women. Cigaritos. Game of monte. Grazing ground. Reconnoissance of General Kearney down the Rio Grande, and appointment of George Bent, Esquire, as Civil Governor. San Domingo and the Puebla Indians. Albuquerque. Armijo. The Priests. Valentia and its vineyards, and soldiers buying fruit of the Indians. Tomae and a religious celebration. A fandango. Return, and bilious fever. Bringing in of Apache chiefs. Making sugar from cornstalks. Wheat harvest. Houses of Indians entered by a ladder. Priestly mummery on the disappearance of the ears of growing corn. Colonel Doniphan goes South. A theatre started by the soldiers. Men picked out to join Colonel Doniphan. Waking in the snow. Author buying corn of a priest. Buying sheep of another who was to catch and deliver them. *Lightning rod.* The Missourian and his "buckram" tents and big wagons. Join Colonel Doniphan. A slight sketch of him. The journey of death. Soap weed. The traders. A Scotchman taken, supposed to be a spy. Three unburied bodies. Sheep, and little flesh upon them.

CHAPTER FOUR

Christmas day. The enemy and a surprise, and the Battle of Bracito. Women in the battle. Alarms. Enter the City of El Paso. The traders do business. Señor Ponce and supplies. Mexican wine and brandy, and the effect of the latter. The priest Ortis. The Scotchman proves to be a scoundrel. Scene of former treachery, and death of a treacherous governor. Apache Indians and their forays. James Kirker. Oxen and mule stolen, and Lieutenant Hinton pursues and brings in a scalp and the stolen animals. Wheat mill made entirely of wood. Mexican cattle; and buying some of a prisoner. Baked pumpkins. Colonel Doniphan and a stolen pig. Bizarre appearance of the troops. Force increased. Presidio del San

Elecario, and a church with its dressed up images. A fat priest and his extortions in a case of marriage.

Chapter Five

A start for Chihuahua. Mail with letters from Santa Fé. Bent's murder, and the true cause of it. Doniphan and the traders. Lake of ducks. A seasonable rain. A warm spring. Carrizal. Wind storm. Another warm spring. Expectation, and an alarm. Grass catches fire and runs up the mountain. Rumor of Mexicans near. Another fire and danger. Enemy not far off. Major Owens takes charge of the wagons. A Mexican spy chased. Picket guard drives in advanced guard of the enemy. Army moves out in solid square. A reconnoitre. The enemy. Doniphan resolves on an attack. The battle of Sacramento; and its results.

Chapter Six

Chihuahua. The bull ring. The Plaza. The Congress Hall. Cathedral. Funeral rites over Major Owens. Mexican naked pet dogs. Chapel of San Francisco. Monument to Hidalgo. Splashes of blood on the pavement. Negro story. Bread, cakes and butter. Architectural freak in building an acqueduct. Dexterity in spinning. Danger among gun powder. The mint. Mr. Potts and his threats. A council called. "Sarah and the children." Start for Parras. Orders to join General Taylor. Difference between rich and poor. Lizards. Rancho and dead bodies. Santa Cruz. The liquor called Mezcal. Guajaquilla. San Berrado. A disappearing spring. Fort Pelayo surprised. Mapini, and the inhabitants' alarm, and Mexican force near. Lights on the mountains. Traders alarmed. Rancho of El Poso and fight with the Lipans. Medicine-man's skull. Parras, and a thief. Brutal attack on a soldier, and Mexican wounded.

138 • CHAPTER ABSTRACTS

CHAPTER SEVEN

Orders to proceed south. San Juan. General Wool, and was there such a man! Battle-field of Buena Vista. Mexican shells. The buried Mexicans. Falsehood of Santa Anna. General Wool and a review. Compliments; and plain speaking. Saltillo. The prettiest girl. Mexican women. A regular soldier's ignorance. Bishop's palace and Monterey. Walnut Springs. General Taylor. Doniphan's account to Taylor of the battle of Sacramento. Leave Walnut Springs. Horrible sight of the remains of the wagon-train suprised by Urrea. Dead Mexican, and how killed. John Smith, a Texian ranger. Brutality of the rangers; and execution of a brave Mexican. Camargo and its canvas houses. A man shot; and revenge. Armadillos, and a story. Description of the soil and its productions. Steamboat seen once again. The Rio Grande and its windings. Burning of saddles, &c. Embarkation and home.